Christ at the Centre

~

Discovering the Cosmic Christ in the spirituality of Bede Griffiths

By

Dr Dion A Forster

Other books by the same Author

A prayer guide for use during examinations

An introduction to Weslyan spirituality

Copyright © 2007 by Dion Forster

ISBN 978-1-920212-24-7

9 781920 212247

Published by:

AcadSA Publishing
PO Box 12322
Edleen, Kempton Park
1625
Rep South Africa

Tel +27 11 976-4044
Fax +27 11 976-4042
info@acadsa.co.za
www.acadsa.co.za

For my Parents

Foreword

Alan Griffiths was born at Walton-on Thames, England in 1906. He was educated at Christ's Hospital and later at Oxford (under the tutelage of C.S. Lewis). At Oxford he read English literature and philosophy. After considerable inner turmoil he came to faith in Christ in 1931 and entered the Roman Catholic Church in 1933. As a novice Benedictine he was given the name Bede, and was finally ordained as a priest 1940. In 1955 Fr Bede went to India to start a Benedictine community with Dom Benedict Alapatt. He later moved to Kurisumala Ashram in Kerala, and finally, in 1968, to  Shantivanam Ashram in Tamil Nadu. He died at Shantivanam in 1993. Fr Bede is regarded by many as a spiritual pioneer. This high regard stems from an appreciation of his spirituality that was rooted in a mystical experience of God. This small book presents and discusses aspects of Fr Bede's cosmic Christology as they arise from his spirituality. This book aims to show how Fr Bede's cosmic Christology that stems from an expression of a real mystical experience of Christ, as the source, sustainer and goal of the whole cosmos, offers both value and insight to Christian spiritual practice and the formulation of doctrine in a new and creative way. What makes Fr Bede's spirituality so valuable is the manner in which he integrated East and West in his spirituality and person, coupled with his ability to draw upon that integration in reflecting and articulating his experience – which ultimately shaped his cosmic Christology. In order to share his knowledge and experience of the cosmic Christ, Fr Bede draws upon linguistic and philosophical concepts from the East (Hinduism in particular) as well as the language and theory arising from discoveries in the areas of quantum physics, microbiology and transpersonal psychology in the West. It is the primacy of spiritual experience, coupled with Fr Bede's ability to integrate the religions, cultures and world-views of the East and West within himself, which makes his cosmic Christology so compelling.

I first came to discover the richness of Fr Bede's spirituality whilst doing my first graduate degree at Rhodes University in Grahamstown, South Africa. There I learned of the richness of Fr Bede's experiential, and practical, spirituality through my mentor and guide, Professor Felicity Edwards. In the late 1990's Fr Bede's books were the cutting edge of an emerging approach to reality and faith – he was among the very first to integrate the 'new science' with perennial philosophy and long accepted Christian doctrine.

I was personally drawn to Fr Bede's spirituality precisely because it was so cutting edge! He managed to hold together diverse realities, such as those of the East and West, the worldviews of science and faith, and through it all he was helping ordinary believers like me to come to a deeper experience of being in Christ.

I have very little doubt that Fr Bede's work will continue to inspire and challenge ordinary Christians and scholars alike. It is my prayer that this little book will add a few words to that conversation.

The original text of this book stems from a Master's degree that I completed in early 2001 at Rhodes University. I have done my best to go through the text and make it less technical and more readable.

Contents

Acknowledgements

As I've indicated in the foreword, I first discovered the value and depth of Fr Bede Griffiths' spirituality while a graduate student at Rhodes University. Through studying his work and attempting to put into practice what I have learnt from him, I have become aware of the important people who have so freely given of their time, energy and expertise to enrich my life. Each of them has made some contribution to this book. Over the last number of years I have developed a love for discovery and reading in the area of contemporary spirituality, not only for the sake of knowledge, but more importantly in a desire to better grasp and understand the truths of spiritual living – what it means to be more fully human in God's sacred world. It is with gratitude to God that I wish to acknowledge the following persons who have contributed to my love and appreciation for Fr Bede and have assisted me in the preparation and presentation of this little book.

Firstly, my thanks to Professor Felicity Edwards who was my supervisor and guide on the original thesis that structured and informed this book. It is her incredible insight and love for spirituality that first encouraged me to study Fr Bede. Her academic ability and knowledge of her subject have inspired me. She truly exemplifies all that a spiritual seeker could hope for in a guide. She is patient, kind and encouraging, a true friend and mentor.

Secondly, I need to acknowledge the Revds George Marchinkowski and Christopher Judelsohn, two of my closest friends and companions in the ministry. George has often offered challenging insights and constructive criticism of my work – he is one of brightest, and most gifted leaders I know. His astute mind and knowledge of Christian theology have challenged me to make discoveries about my own faith and the doctrines that inform it. Christopher, through his incredible pastoral ability and passion for people, has inspired me in my ministry. His giftedness and ability to share a living faith with those around him have constantly challenged me to 'keep my head out of the clouds' and my 'feet on the ground.'

Then also I wish to honour my friend Dr Kevin Snyman who walked this spiritual path long before I discovered it. His courage and faith opened the way for me to follow.

Thirdly, I give thanks to my colleagues and fellow Christians in the Methodist Church of Southern Africa who have allowed me the freedom to explore my faith and develop a fairly eclectic theology. I am particularly indebted to the students and staff John Wesley College (the seminary of the Methodist church of Southern Africa), who give me the space to form and test my thoughts. Thank you to my colleagues Prof Neville Richardson, Rev Madika Sibeko, and Rev Ruth Jonas for their challenge, encouragement, and friendship. I must also make special mention of my close friend Dr Wessel Bentley a great scholar and friend, whose theology is so much better than mine! Wessel reads my work with critical interest and is honest enough to challenge what needs changing, and sharpen what is dull. Spirituality is formed in community and this one is no different. It bears the marks of three further Christian communities, the student community of Rhodes University (where I did most of my graduate work), the Coronation Ave Methodist Church in Cape Town (that I pastored for 5 years), and the loving acceptance of the Bryanston Methodist Church that has been my home since 2004 – I still preach at Bryanston most Sunday evenings. It never ceases to amaze me that people actually turn up to listen!

I especially need to thank the Revd Brian Hazell and Mrs Hilbre Currin for assisting me to sharpen my appalling grammar, and in so doing helped me put my fledgling thoughts into words with greater accuracy. There is no doubt that as the astute reader thumbs the pages of this book, she or he will find both errors in presentation and content – I am always pleased to be helped along and shown my error! So please do feel free to send me a message with suggestions, changes, and corrections. You'll find my email address and web address at the end of these acknowledgements.

Finally, and most importantly, I want to thank my wife, Megan. She has sacrificed a great deal of our time together as I wrote and edited this manuscript. Her patience in allowing me to engage in my love of putting my thoughts and feelings into words is appreciated so very much! Megan is truly a gift form God! I know few people as faithful and committed to Christ. She is a wonderful mother to our miracle children, Courtney and Liam, and an inspiring and loving companion. I could not dream of any better! I am grateful for her loving support – I love her deeply.

Dion Forster
John Wesley College, Pretoria (2007)
http://www.spirituality.org.za
dion@spirituality.org.za

Chapter 1

Mystical experience - The context that shaped Fr Bede's spirituality

Karl Rahner, one of the most prominent Catholic theologians of our time, once commented that the "... Christian of the future will be a mystic or he or she will not exist at all" (in Schneiders 1990:677). This statement serves as a poignant reminder that doctrinal accuracy alone (i.e., believing the 'right things') will never secure the survival of the Christian faith. The truth that Rahner summed up so succinctly is of course that there can be no *expression* of the mystery of God if there is no *experience* of the mysterious God. However, there is one further point that needs to be made, that is that there can be no experience of God if there is no mystical approach to the mystery of God. It is the primary emphasis on experience that makes the mystic better able to adapt his or her faith to cope with the challenges of an ever changing world – after all, even when everything changes around one, the experience of the divine mystery will always remain the same, a mystery.

Throughout Fr Bede Griffiths' life, as a Benedictine monk (both in England and India), spiritual experience always took priority over doctrinal formulation in his spirituality. Within the context of this little book it can safely be said that for him the experience of Christ was much more important than a water tight expression of the doctrine of Christ. In Fr Bede's spirituality one comes to discover that this experience was beyond one culture, one language, one philosophy – and even, one religion. As we shall see, Fr Bede's experience of Christ was primarily, although not exclusively, cosmic in nature. His cosmic Christology, as it is recorded in his many works, arose from a desire to share the truth and excitement of his discovery with those with whom he came into contact. Thus, Fr Bede's aim in writing and teaching was not so much to articulate the doctrine of the cosmic Christ as it was to articulate and share his own mystical experience of the reality of Christ, and to communicate the significance of that reality for the whole cosmos or created order.

This little book will present what I believe to be the most significant aspects of Fr Bede's cosmic Christology as I have come to understand them from studying his spirituality. While many of the aspects of his cosmic Christology are not new to the doctrine of Christ, in the sense of being completely unique, they are extremely valuable in that they stem from his spiritual experience and are filtered through his context and character. However, there are some cases in which Fr Bede has drawn upon, and applied, previously unused concepts in expressing his cosmic Christology. Thus, one can say that his Christology has a unique or personal 'flavour' to it. I hope that you will come to appreciate this wonderfully unique 'flavour'! If properly engaged with it can be of great value for spiritual experience and doctrinal formulation in future works of Christian doctrine, and in the development of novel approaches to Christian spirituality.

Fr Bede's spirituality, and subsequent theological reflection upon that spiritual experience, were fundamentally shaped and enriched by the context in which he lived out his faith , and in particular we will see how his spirituality and theology were shaped by the years he spent as a monk living in India. This rich life's experience (discussed in chapter two) allowed Fr Bede to operate within the conceptual frameworks of both eastern and western culture, and philosophy. Thus, unlike many other Christologies, Fr Bede's Christology is able to draw on the positive aspects of both eastern and western culture, leading to a far more culturally balanced and contextually honest Christology. In this little book I hope to show the value of applying philosophical and linguistic concepts that were previously unused in Christology, and how such approaches, if carefully applied, can enrich our devotion toward, and understanding of, Jesus. Indeed, I intend to suggest that such an integrative Christology can be of global significance, since approaching the doctrine of Christ in this manner supersedes boundaries created by drawing on only one culture and one set of philosophical and linguistic concepts. The principles that one can learn from Fr Bede's approach can be of value to Christians throughout the world who long to see some fresh and novel approaches to Christology that differ from the traditionally Western theologies that tend to dominate modern Christian thought and scholarship.

Fr Bede's spirituality is integrative in nature. What exactly does this mean? Well, it will be shown that his spirituality encouraged him to integrate and move beyond some of the limitations of traditional language and philosophy we use when talking about Jesus. Stemming from this one is able to see a greater harmony between a mystical approach to God, as found in the East, and the pragmatic and social approach as found in western spiritualities. This approach reflects one of his primary spiritual aims, that is, to establish a marriage between East and West – an integration of the best of eastern and western approaches to the mystery of God (cf. Griffiths 1982:40; 1989:296).

Bede Griffiths' integrative approach makes his Christology much more acceptable to the eastern mind, through its application and integration of eastern linguistic concepts and philosophy, while at the same time serving as an important corrective to some of the dualities found in modern western society and religion. Most notable amongst these dualities is the radical dualism that the West places between creation and creator. We shall see that this dualism can be found in many forms of western religion and secular culture. Gaining a clearer understanding of how an experiential, or spiritual, Christology can achieve the aims of overarching integration is of importance to Christian scholars as well, since it will help us to understand how future challenges to doctrine may be encountered through mystical or spiritual experience.

So this discussion of Fr Bede's cosmic Christology will serve to show how a doctrinal formulation that arises from spirituality can add valuable insight for both Christian doctrine and practice. The structure of the book is as follows: Firstly, since Fr Bede's context radically affects his spirituality, the next chapter will highlight some formative spiritual events that shaped and informed his spirituality. Chapter three presents a more in depth discussion of the philosophical and theological concepts that arise from his experience. We will see that these spiritual experiences form the background to his cosmic Christology. In chapter four some aspects of Fr Bede's cosmic Christology are discussed in detail. These are aspects that are seen to offer creative insights while enriching the continuing development of the doctrine of Christ. The next chapter draws on these insights and shows in a specific way what contribution Fr Bede's cosmic Christology can make to Christian spiritual experience and theological discourse. The book concludes with a brief summary and selected comments on Fr Bede's spirituality. Some of the terminology and words used in this book may be unknown to those who are not familiar with Indian philosophy and Hindu religion. Please refer to the glossary of terms at the end of this book if you are unsure of any of the terminology used in the text.

Chapter 2

A journey towards the centre - The marriage of East and West in the life of Bede Griffiths

Theology, faith, and most importantly spirituality, take shape in the lives of people as they live, interact, and come to discover more and more of the mystery of God's nature. I am convinced that Bede Griffiths' spirituality is primarily based upon his experience of God, this is a dynamic and changing experience that adapted as his context changed. Thus, any discussion of Fr Bede's spirituality would need to discuss and highlight some of the important and formative experiences that comprise the rich tapestry of his life. The section that follows will do that, although selectively. It would be an impossible task, and certainly one that is way beyond the scope of this book, to point to all of the important experiences and changes that Fr Bede went through in his life. Rather, the intent here is to give some insight into who Fr Bede was, and how his spiritual experiences helped him formulate his cosmic Christology in particular. There are some truly excellent biographies that will help those who wish to know more about Fr Bede's life and experience than can be discussed here.[1] The first part of this discussion will draw connections between historical events in his life and his emerging faith. However, once Fr Bede reaches the shores of India the changes are much more radical, and much less simplistically linkable to historic events. This latter section of his life will take the form a discussion on how Fr Bede appropriated and understood himself as a Hindu-Christian sannyasi.

Anglican to agnostic, agnostic to Catholic, Catholic to Christian sannyasi

Bede Griffiths went to India in 1955 where he lived until his death on the 13th of May 1993. He was born Alan Griffiths on 17 December 1906 in Walton on Thames in England, where he was raised as a member of the Church of England (Griffiths 1979:18).

Alan's upbringing was thoroughly English, an aspect of his person that would affect the rest of his life, according to those who knew him. He was educated at Christ's Hospital. Here he became interested in the literary works of the great English and classical writers that would later be instrumental in his conversion to the Christian faith (Spink 1988:44). It was at Christ's Hospital that Alan had his first truly religious experience, which interestingly enough, took place in nature (cf. Griffiths 1979:9-12). Fr Bede relates in the video, *A human search: the life of Fr Bede Griffiths* (1993), that while walking one evening he was suddenly overwhelmed by the beauty of nature as if he realised the power of God for the first time. In reflecting on this awesome experience of God in nature, Fr Bede describes it as his first awakening to "cosmic" religion. Although, at the time, he sensed that these feelings had "something of a religious character" to them, he had no interest whatsoever in any sort of formal religion (cf. du Boulay 1998:16). Such a desire would surface only later in his life.

Alan Griffiths entered Magdalen College, Oxford, in 1925 and soon came under the tutelage of C.S. Lewis[2], who had a marked effect on Fr Bede's spiritual and academic development. At Oxford, according to Fr Bede, his love for nature grew to become his only religion (Griffiths 1979:10). Fr Bede reflects that it was only years later that he came to realise that the love and power that he had experienced that day in nature at Christ's Hospital emanated from the same God who was preached about in Christianity (Griffiths 1979:130). While at Oxford, Alan Griffiths met two significant people, Hugh Waterman and Martyn Skinner, whose friendship would be a "constant thread through Alan's life... corresponding regularly until the end of their lives" (du Boulay 1998:20). They all shared the same view that 'modern' society had lost its sense of the sacred – I am fairly certain that it is this particular insight that draws so many contemporary seekers to Fr Bede's integrative spirituality (Spink 1988:54). Fr Bede was later to make this one of the central emphases in his spirituality, seeking to correct the modern secular western world-view with the mystical world-view of the East. However, in the pre-Indian stage of his life Alan, together with these two men, attempted to overcome this loss of the sacred in society by entering into a social experiment of withdrawing from modern industrialised English society and engaging in living a common life in the countryside. While this experiment in the Cotswolds did little to appease his dissatisfaction with western society, it was nonetheless a valuable and formative period. This time in Alan's life can be characterised as a stage of philosophical and spiritual discovery as he undertook a concentrated 'diet' of seventeenth and eighteenth century literature. Included in this 'reading diet' was the Black Letter edition of the Authorised version of the Bible – which he initially approached as purely literary study. However, Alan soon began to find that the "reconciliation of religion and philosophy which he had glimpsed in Dante and St Augustine had its root in the Old Testament itself" (du Boulay 1998:51). Du Boulay notes an important shift in Alan during this stage, recounting that soon "Hugh and Alan passed from reading to praying, dropping to their knees" (du Boulay 1998:51). Although correspondence around that time confirms that they did not consider themselves Christians, there can be little doubt that Alan had begun to experience an awakening to the Christian faith (du Boulay 1998:52)

In the months following this experience in 1931, along with continued contact with C.S. Lewis, Alan began to discover Christianity more acutely (cf. du Boulay 1998:60-61). It was during this time of intense struggle and confusion that Alan felt the need to spend a whole day in prayer. While praying, he saw himself at the foot of the cross of Christ and in this visionary state he surrendered himself to the Lordship of Christ. Of course this was a seminal shift in his conversion to Christ, and a significant milestone in the development of his faith. Once he had fully associated himself with the Christian faith it was less than a month before he entered monastic life at Prinknash Abbey. He became a novice there on 20 December 1933. After making his Simple Profession (21 December 1934) and Solemn Profession (21 December 1937) he studied philosophy and theology before being ordained as a priest on the 9th of March 1940 (Griffiths 1979:168).

Fr Bede notes in the video *A human search: the life of Fr Bede Griffiths* (1993) that his profound interest in religions of the East came as a result of the writings of Christopher Dawson which he discovered during this phase of his life[3]. From this time on he began to study Chinese and Indian religion in earnest, and was introduced to the practice of yoga by the Jungian analyst, Tony Sussman. He became convinced, as had others before him, that if the Christian religion was ever to penetrate the East, it must be interpreted into eastern categories to make it intelligible to the eastern mind (Rajan 1989:102). This realisation would have a profound effect upon the way in which Fr Bede later lived and expressed his spirituality in India. It was, however, only in 1955 that Fr Bede had an opportunity to go to India himself. This opportunity came at the request of Dom Benedict Alapatt, an Indian Benedictine monk, who had asked him to assist in the establishment of an Indian Benedictine monastery in Kengeri, Banglore.

Initially Fr Bede had no intention of changing his lifestyle from the accepted Benedictine practice and standards. He wore a traditional habit and built a western style chapel with chairs and reading desks. The cells of the monastery were simply furnished with wooden beds and straw mattresses. Gradually however he began to realise that what he regarded as poverty (as a westernised Benedictine monk) was in fact luxury compared to the ordinary way of life in the neighbouring village (Griffiths 1982:13). In the nearby villages it was common practice to sleep on the floor, eat meals with one's hands and to go barefoot. The 'simple' lifestyle that the monks were living was considered one of comfort compared to that of most Indians. Hence, Fr Bede recalls that he slowly began to reject these western practices in order to "come nearer to the condition of the poor man in India" (1982:18). Throughout his ministry Fr Bede constantly sought to enter into the experience of those among whom he lived and worked.

A further step of inculturation took place in March 1958 when Fr Bede, together with a Belgian monk, Fr Mahieu, founded Kurisumala Ashram (Mountain of the Cross) at Kerala. Ashram life was based on utter simplicity. Fr Mahieu had come to India in order to reveal the contemplative nature of the Catholic Church to Indians and felt that his task could best be performed in the formation of an ashram that combined advaitic (Hindu, non dualistic) and Christian traditions of contemplation (Rajan 1989:106). This was the first time that the concept of advaitic sannyasa had been incorporated into Christian monastic life (Rajan 1989:102). In this regard Fr Bede writes:

> It was our desire to enter into this tradition of Indian sannyasa and to establish a Christian ashram, in which the life of prayer and asceticism could be followed along Christian lines, yet keeping always in touch with the traditions of India (Griffiths in Rajan 1989:107).

At Kurisumala the Benedictine rule was followed with a strict Cistercian observance to complement the contemplative emphasis of the eastern traditions. Fr Bede stayed here for ten years. In 1968 he moved to Shantivanam Ashram (meaning 'Forest of Peace') in Tamil Nadu to take over from one of the founders of the ashram, Dom Henri le Saux[4] (Abhishiktananda). Fr le Saux had been deeply influenced by the contemplative life of India. He would retreat to his hermitage in a cave on Mount Arunachula whenever possible and eventually left Shantivanam altogether for a life of solitude and contemplation.

Fr Bede comments on the significance of the change and inculturation that took place as a result of his move to Shantivanam, saying, "Here we were able to start our monastic life again in a more radical way... now I embarked on something different" (Griffiths 1989:24). At Shantivanam Fr Bede was able to enter more deliberately into the contemplative life of the East.

Life at the Ashram was truly ecumenical (in the broader, inter-religious, sense of the word). There were times of structured prayer and meditation, as well as reading from the scriptures of the different religions. Fr Bede describes the religious life of the community as follows:

> ... we meet for prayer three times a day, not for the formal prayer of the liturgy as at Kurisumala, but for more informal prayer... as well as readings from the Bible... In the morning we read from the Vedas, at midday from the Koran... (Griffiths 1982:24).

A further innovation to religious life at Shantivanam was the way in which the Eucharist was celebrated. Following the concessions of

Vatican II, the liturgy and elements used for the Eucharist were adapted in order to make them more culturally accessible to the Indian mindset.

From an ecumenical point of view what Fr Bede was aiming to achieve here was a fulfilment of true sannyasa (further on in this chapter there is a brief introduction to the concept of sannyasa), where the sannyasi is in essence beyond all religious divisions, seeking to move beyond the limits of one set of cultural, philosophical or religious symbols, aiming only to attain pure *advaita* (non-duality) (Spink 1988:154; there is also a brief discussion of *advaita* later in this chapter). This emphasis on going beyond the concepts and symbols of religion to an experience of the reality that they represent was an essential element of Fr Bede's spirituality[5]. It will be suggested, later in chapter five, that Fr Bede saw language, doctrine and philosophy as inadequate to fully capture the truth of an experience of God. As a consequence, these aspects of the faith had to be integrated and transcended in a quest for spiritual truth.

One further aspect of Fr Bede's spiritual life that significantly influenced his spirituality was his relationship to the pilgrims and ashramites at Shantivanam. Rajan says that many of Fr Bede's disciples regarded him as a spiritual guide, and in some cases even as their guru (1989:102). However, from conversations with Professor Edwards, who knew Fr Bede personally (and edited a number of his books), it would seem that he never regarded himself as a guru in the technical sense of the concept, but rather as a teacher (*acharya*). The Hindu guru has the awesome task of taking responsibility for the salvation of his disciples. For this reason, Fr Bede spoke of Christ as being the only true guru (*sadguru*), the only one who could truly save anyone from his or her sins. It is nonetheless true that he fulfilled a very important spiritual role for many through his teaching and spiritual discipline. Moreover his spirituality served not only to teach and guide many spiritual pilgrims but also served as an example of his commitment to fostering a contextually honest spirituality.

Fr Bede stayed at Shantivanam, living as a Christian sannyasi, until his death on 13 May 1993.

Fr Bede as Christian sannyasi.

It is important to devote some of this discussion of experience, context, and history, to examining Fr Bede as a Christian sannyasi. Fr Bede's life as a sannyasi affects not only the way in which he lived out his faith, but also the manner in which he expressed his spiritual experiences. Accordingly, this aspect of his life and spirituality has a profound effect on his cosmic Christology.

Before discussing Fr Bede as a sannyasi I will give a brief outline of the concept of sannyasa in India.

A brief description of sannyasa.

The most basic description of the concept of sannyasa is to describe it as total abandonment. The word *sannyasa* is often transliterated as *samnyāsa*. However, in English literary texts, and many of Fr Bede's own works, it is anglicised as sannyasa. The word sannyasa is composed of the prefix *sam* which means totally or wholeheartedly, and the verb *nyasa* meaning to lay aside, resign or abandon (Rajan 1989:10).

Therefore the sannyasi is a person who completely abandons every care, need and concern for the world, self and others in order to attain realisation of the Supreme Self. The person who chooses this rigorous ascetic life of poverty and exploration for Self-realisation is called a *sannyasin*. Sannyasa, as an *ashrama,* is the best means of *brahmavidya* (knowledge of Brahman) (cf. Abhishiktananda 1984:3). Commonly sannyasa is the fourth *ashrama* or stage of one's journey to Self-realisation. In traditional Indian life there are commonly four *ashrama*: *brahmacharya* (studentship), *grhastha* (householder), *vanaprastha* (forest hermit) and lastly *sannyasa,* the stage of renunciation (Vattakuzhy 1981:14-17). After a person has completed their duty (*rsis*) by passing through the first three *ashrama* he is able to make a break with the past in pursuit of *moksa* (final liberation or salvation). However, old age or completion of the first three *ashrama* is not a pre-requisite for sannyasa. At any stage in one's life a person could at will withdraw from all worldly pursuits, cutting short, or leaving out, the preceding stages altogether to enter into sannyasa (Vattakuzhy 1981:18). All that is necessary is a desire for complete detachment from everything in order to foster an intense attachment to the divine.

The person who completes the ritual initiation into sannyasa (*sannyasa diksha*) is "expected to be free from all bonds in the world in order to be a visible witness to the transcendence of God" (Rajan 1989:23). As Father Bede says, a sannyasi is

> ...called to go beyond all religion, beyond every human institution, beyond every scripture or creed, till he comes to that which every religion and scripture and ritual signifies but can never name... the Sannyasi is one who is called to go beyond all religion and seek that ultimate goal (Griffiths 1982:43).

The values of the life of sannyasa are: absolute poverty, complete solitude and silence, and universal love and equanimity, as well as contemplation and prayer in order to realise the divine. Sannyasis are regarded as dead to society because of their total renunciation. Rajan notes that when a person is initiated into sannyasa, his kinsmen perform the ceremonies and rites for death (*atyesthi*) (Rajan 1989:25). When the sannyasi dies his physical death is commemorated using a different ceremony called *samadhi*.

Christian adoption of sannyasa and Fr Bede's interpretation of it.

The Christian monastic life and the life of the Indian sannyasi are in many ways similar, and in many others dissimilar. Rajan suggests that both share a common aim, that is, to reach the consciousness of the Ultimate Reality, or God (1989:160). From a Christian perspective Conner suggests that it is the purpose of every person, and more so the monk or contemplative, to return to "that original unity from which we have strayed, in order to restore the 'image' in which we were created" (1996:81). Here it can be seen that in sannyasa there is a common meeting point between Christianity and Hinduism.

This contemplative and unitive desire was observed by some early Christians who came to India, such as Roberto De Nobili who arrived in India in May 1605, and is believed to be the first Christian to have adopted sannyasa. Initially sannyasa was outwardly incorporated into Christianity as a means of making this faith more culturally acceptable to the Hindu (Rajan 1989:71). By adopting the lifestyle of the Indian holy person in the matter of dress, diet and manner of living, the Christian sannyasi was able to engage more effectively in mission work. At this stage, the aim, in almost all cases, was to convert Indian people to the Christian faith by proclamation of the gospel accompanied by social action.

Later, however, with the arrival of Christians such as Jules Monchanin (Swami Parama Arubi Anandam) and Henri Le Saux (Abhishiktananda), the aim changed considerably. The deeply contemplative nature of sannyasa was realised as were the benefits that sannyasa would have for the Christian faith. This is a notable shift. It displays a shift from a desire to impart the Christian faith to India, to a desire to enrich the Christian faith by learning from the religion and philosophy of India. During this stage there was a greater realisation that the *advaitic* experience (i.e. the non-dual experience of God beyond name and form) and devotion to Christ could co-exist and assist the Christian devotee in attaining the goal of realising the Ultimate Reality. This stemmed from the recognition that India was already deeply spiritual, and that this spirituality could be of benefit to the Christian faith (Rajan 1989:88). This latter view is much closer to Fr Bede's motivation for entering sannyasa, than the former view of evangelical mission.

The emphasis of the Christian sannyasi thus shifted from a one-sided desire to proclaim a culturally acceptable version of the Gospel, to a mutually enriching emphasis on contemplation. Rajan writes:

> Abhishiktananda asserts that a Christian *sannyasin* who would devote himself to be a witness to the Absolute can effectively spread the message of the Gospel. A widely spread Christian *sannyasa* would prove to the Hindus that the Church is primarily a spiritual reality and that her selfless social service through various organisations and institutions is subservient to her essential function of contemplation (Rajan 1989:93).

One of the major differences between the Christian sannyasin and the Hindu sannyasin is that the Christian sannyasin is often linked to an ashram or monastic community, whereas the Hindu sannyasin is traditionally a wandering ascetic, since sannyasa in Hinduism implies renunciation of all things – even the necessity for community. This difference, in Christianity, has been justified by suggesting a reapplication of an authentic approach to non-attachment (particularly in relation to possessions). As Fr Bede puts it,

> [t]his is the real renunciation which is demanded, the
> renunciation of 'I' and 'mine'... detachment is the key
> word. It does not matter so much what material
> possessions you have, so long as you are not attached to
> them (Griffiths 1976:11).

The aim of the Christian sannyasi was thus to detach oneself from all
things, as a spiritual discipline that can take place within community,
and to establish a form of contemplative life based on the traditions of
Christian monasticism and Hindu sannyasa.

> Christian sannyasa is essentially a spiritual reality, a
> living experience in the Spirit of Divine Love. Its source
> is nothing other than the inner experience of the
> Incarnate Word who in its constant unveiling
> phenomenon makes sannyasa a potent means of making
> God's love available to all.... Jesus' union with the father
> and the dedication to his fellow-beings, both lived
> through the Holy Spirit, is the model for Christian
> sannyasa.... Thus the life of Christian sannyasa consists
> of two-fold experiences; experience of God and
> experience of human communion (Aykara in Rajan
> 1989:190).

It is in this sense that Fr Bede was a Christian sannyasi. For Fr Bede,
sannyasa was not just a way of life or some form of religious order;
rather it was a matter of 'being' (an ontological state), and as such, far
more than just the action of complete renunciation. It is only after utter
renunciation of all, even sannyasa (or renunciation) itself, when the
experience of the divine is realised in the centre of one's being, that
one begins to grasp what living as a sannyasin means (cf. Rajan
1989:113).

From an early stage Fr Bede began to realise that western thought
and practice, which dominates most of the modern world, was
inadequate. It made up only half of the truth. An overemphasis on
Cartesian philosophy and Newtonian physics, along with the western
emphasis on reason, was leading humanity astray. In essence the
West's complete dependence upon reason and science makes it a
prisoner to the limitations of language, symbol, quantity, philosophy,
and human reason. This has contributed towards a world-view that
makes existence profane, robbing it of the mystery of the sacred. Fr
Bede relates:

> I had begun to find that there was something lacking not only in the Western world but in the Western Church. We were living from one half of our soul, from the conscious, rational level and we needed to discover the other half, the unconscious intuitive dimension. I wanted to experience in my life the marriage of these two dimensions of human existence, the rational and the intuitive, the conscious and the unconscious, the masculine and the feminine. I wanted to find the way to the marriage of East and West (Griffiths 1982:8).

It was through his exposure to the Hindu notion of *advaita*, in particular, and through his life as a Christian in India, that Fr Bede began to discover the marriage, he refers to above, and strive for a non-dual existence. In the West the masculine aspect is dominant and is characterised by aggressive power, rational thought, and deductive science. In the East, on the other hand, the feminine is dominant, and can be associated with features such as sympathetic power, an intuitive mind and the perennial philosophy. For Fr Bede it was only a marriage between these two that would save the world from ultimate destruction (cf. Griffiths 1982:40; 1989:296).

Through his lifestyle as a sannyasi, that is, a lifestyle characterised by contemplation, simplicity and complete renunciation, the marriage of East and West became a reality for Fr Bede. As sannyasi he aimed to transcend East and West, masculine and feminine, reason and intuition, to reach the one Reality, the reality that is the source of everything. This Ultimate Reality escapes all explanation. It can be experienced only in the depth of one's being. According to the Chandogya Upanishad VI:2. 1-4 it is "beneath and beyond all multiplicity". The Absolute is the source of both East and West, the masculine and the feminine, of reason and intuition. Here all things are One (cf. Ephesians 1:10 and Rajan 1989:115). This realisation is consciousness of the Absolute. This is what true sannyasa makes possible – the transcendence of all religion, all creeds, all spiritual exercises and rituals (Griffiths 1982:42). It is here that one discovers the True Self, where the I-Thou separation breaks down between the person and God. It is difficult to formulate such non-dual constructs from a purely western mind-set. The eastern mind-set, which is far more intuitive than rational, allows for a greater understanding of Reality in this sense.

> This is the great discovery of Indian thought, the
> discovery of the Self, the Atman, the Ground of personal
> being, which is one with Brahman, the Ground of
> universal being (Griffiths 1984:16).

It is my conclusion that sannyasa, not as a manner of living but as a
way of being, brought Fr Bede to an experience of what it means to be
truly Christian. It is important to note at this point that as a sannyasin
one does not reject the things renounced (such as one's religion and
values); rather these are integrated as part of who and what one is. Just
like a letter is not rejected when one transcends it by incorporating it
into a word, neither is a word rejected when it is formed into a
sentence, or a sentence when it forms a book. Each is valuable,
necessary, and exists as a part within the greater whole. Every stage in
one's life is a significant part of true Self-realisation. In a sense one has
to pass beyond the 'symbols' used in religion to the reality that it
represents. The symbols contain and convey something of the reality
that they signify. The symbols are therefore to be integrated into one's
spirituality as one moves towards a greater realisation of the truth,
since they are not a 'false' reality, merely an attempt at representing the
true reality. The symbols of a religion are not to be regarded as the
religion itself, but to be transcended in order to discover why the
religion exists.

Conclusion

The experiences of life significantly influence and impact on one's
spirituality and subsequent expression thereof. Taking this into
account, this section aimed to give some insight into Fr Bede's
spiritual development and the significant aspects of his life and
spiritual experience; showing how these shaped and gave rise to his
spirituality, and so too, his cosmic Christology. The essential
elements of the above discussion have shown how Fr Bede's
spirituality began and ended beyond the commonly accepted
boundaries of the Christian faith. It is notable that his spirituality
began at Christ's Hospital with a 'cosmic' awakening to God in
nature (cf. Griffiths 1979:9-12), and ended with a highly developed
understanding of the cosmic Christ, through his contemplative life
as a sannyasi[6]. As a sannyasi, Fr Bede constantly sought to integrate
and transcend the symbols of religion in order to discover the One

True Source of all reality that lies beyond all religious expressions and structures. Out of this he was able to develop a cosmic Christology that is based not just on the doctrinal and philosophical formulations of one religion, but to move beyond those names and forms to an experience of Christ as both the source and goal of the whole cosmos. One of Fr Bede's favourite passages from the Svetasvatara Upanishad outlines his understanding of the cosmic Christ in this regard so well.

> I know that Great Person of the brightness of the sun beyond the darkness. Only by knowing him one goes beyond death, there is no other way to go. (Svetasvatara Upanishad III:8).

Chapter 3

The philosophical and theological background to Bede Griffiths' cosmic Christology

The previous chapter discussed some of the more significant experiences in Fr Bede's life that informed and developed his unique spirituality. However, Fr Bede's spirituality does not end with experience, he was also an effective and creative communicator and teacher who endeavoured to share his discoveries of truth with others in symbols, words, and concepts, that could appeal to the contemporary mindset. Naturally any process of communication requires the use of language, symbols, and conceptual frameworks to communicate what has been discovered in. This chapter of the book will discuss Fr Bede's understanding, and use of, particular theological and philosophical concepts that underpin his cosmic Christology.

A primary focus that arises from Fr Bede's mystical spirituality is the relationship between God and God's creation (traditionally referred to as the created order), namely that God and creation are not radically separated from one another (even though they are significantly different, they are nonetheless one). This conclusion can be clearly surmised from Fr Bede's desire to overcome any artificial dualities (*dvaita*) that tend to arise between Creator and creation in so many western Christian theologies. The doctrine of the cosmic Christ, as expressed by Fr Bede, is a clear example of this non-dual (advaitic) relationship between creator and creation. It is in his theology of the cosmic Christ that the discussion of the relationship between the absolute and the contingent takes shape and is articulated with the greatest accuracy, or at least as much accuracy as one can muster within the symbolic and conceptual frameworks of language. Since this book is discussing a theology that arises from a reflection upon spiritual experience, it is important to scrutinise the philosophical and theological background that Fr Bede employs in expressing his doctrine of the cosmic Christ. An understanding of how he utilises theological and philosophical concepts and terms will lend a fuller understanding of both his experience of the cosmic Christ and its significance for others.

The discussion that follows will focus on three areas in particular: firstly, Fr Bede's understanding of revelation as both general and particular; secondly, there will be a brief discussion of what Fr Bede accepted as the three primary aspects of reality; namely, the physical, spiritual and psychological; finally, this chapter will conclude with a section that outlines Fr Bede's 'new vision of reality'. In order to do justice to Fr Bede's 'new vision of reality' it will be necessary to make reference to some developments in contemporary scholarship from disciplines other theology and philosophy. In particular it will be necessary to consider developments in the 'new science' since these had a significant impact upon Fr Bede's spiritual paradigm – in a sense the linguistic and philosophical framework of the new science gave him a wider vocabulary to use in articulating his cosmic Christology.

Revelation

To comprehend Fr Bede's concept of the cosmic Christ it is necessary, firstly, to consider his understanding of how God reveals God's self to the created order. For Fr Bede revelation takes place in two stages (Griffiths 1992:95). Firstly, he affirms that God's revelation began before Christianity (as a religion) entered history, and thus God also revealed God's self before the historical event of the incarnation of Christ. This type of revelation, he suggested, takes place in a cosmic religion, that is, ancient cultures and people became aware that there is a sense of the sacred which is present in animals, plants, the earth, the sun, humans, in fact, in all creation (Griffiths 1992:95). This is the first stage of revelation and it is aptly called the cosmic revelation. This understanding is not unique to Fr Bede, in fact many perennialist theologians and philosophers hold the same view. In fact, this view is vital to the resurgence of interest in primal cultures and religions in post colonial Africa, Asia, and South America.

The second stage of revelation, which is also an aspect of the cosmic revelation, is far more particular and is very much like the revelation of God contained in the sacred texts of the world's religions. This revelation was gradually expressed, formulated, and articulated as people developed their use of language and symbols and began to use their powers of discrimination in relation to the Truth contained in all reality, particularly as it is related to places, events, contextual concerns, and particular people of religious and cultural importance (Griffiths 1982:89). Fr Bede refers to this second stage of revelation as a distinct movement within the cosmic revelation because of its close ties to history and culture (1982:175-176). A more detailed discussion of Fr Bede's understanding and appropriation of these two forms of revelation follows below.

General or cosmic revelation

This section is concerned with general or 'cosmic revelation', the first stage mentioned above. Fr Bede speaks of it as, "... the revelation of ultimate Truth, given to all mankind through the Cosmos, that is, through the creation" (Griffiths 1982:88). In this sense, then, Fr Bede speaks of the whole of creation as a theophany or manifestation and revelation of God. However, as a Christian, he points out that this revelation finds its clearest and most accurate expression in the person of Christ.

> The Father manifests himself in his Son or Word, who by taking our human flesh assumes the whole creation to himself and fills it with his presence (Eph 4:10). We cannot properly speaking think of anything apart from Christ; it is he who gives existence its meaning (Griffiths 1984:219).

Thus, whereas many other perennialist philosophers and theologians would agree that all of creation is in some sense a 'theophany' (an expression of God), Fr Bede goes further referring to the whole of creation not only as a theophany, but also as a "Christophany" (Griffiths 1984:219). This emphasis highlights an interesting and complex aspect of Fr Bede's spirituality. Throughout his lectures and writings he is concerned, on the one hand, to relate all of his discoveries to the Christian faith. On the other hand, however, he points out that these experiences are valid not because they are Christian, rather their authenticity is as a result of their cosmic nature. They are experiences that transcend any single expression of faith or religion. A cosmic experience could thus find expression within the symbols and conceptual frameworks of a particular faith, however, that faith could not claim the unique and exclusive rights to that experience. A person of another faith could, for example, have the same experience of the divine and express it using different symbols and conceptual frameworks that are more suitable to his or her religious convictions. The expression is secondary to the experience.

So, having made this point, Fr Bede goes on to say that he "began to see how all religion had grown from a perception of an all-pervading spirit which was held to be present in all phenomena" (Griffiths 1995:vii). While this spirit, or power, was very often conceived as one (i.e., non-dual, or undivided), it was often considered to manifest in many varied forms. These manifestations of the divine were variously regarded as gods and goddesses, angels and spirits, ancestors and spiritual forces (cf. Griffiths 1995:viii). The understanding of these manifestations came to be expressed in the myths and legends of cosmic religions that predate Christianity. Fr Bede explains the importance of these myths in cosmic religion and revelation as follows:

> A myth is a symbolic story which expresses, in symbolic terms which rise from the depths of the unconscious, man's understanding of God and the mystery of existence. Myths are of infinite value and importance. I do not think it is too strong to say that God revealed Himself from the earliest times in the form of myth.... Every religion is derived from mythology... (Griffiths 1983:115).

This kind of general or cosmic revelation predates the 'particular revelation' of God that is commonly found in contemporary formalised religion. It is, rather, the foundation from which particular revelation stems. Wong notes that, "cosmic revelation is based on the belief that God reveals himself in creation and the human soul" (1996:1). This concept is not foreign in Christianity – in fact the Apostle Paul speaks of just such a revelation in Romans 1:20 when he writes that "... since the creation of the world God's invisible qualities—his eternal power and divine nature—have been clearly seen, being understood from what has been made..." (NIV).

Pertaining to this form of universal or cosmic revelation, the cosmic Person would be that person who underlies, or is manifest in, all creation as the one who creates and gives meaning to all creation. Fr Bede understood this person to be Jesus Christ. As seen above, Fr Bede understood that all creation was not only a general 'theophany', but in fact a 'Christophany'. The whole of creation finds its meaning and purpose in Christ because in the incarnation God enters the created order. Moreover, in the ascension Christ assumes, or representatively takes, the whole material universe into the Godhead – since Jesus, as a fully human person takes the matter of his bodily existence into the Trinitarian life of God. The conclusion of this understanding is thus, not only that God is seen in the whole of creation, but that the whole of creation is seen in God – while there is radical distinction between the nature of Creator and creation, there is no radical dualism, the two are radically one. In making this point, and wanting to show that it is not foreign to traditional Christian theology, Fr Bede quotes (1989:171) Meister Eckhart who wrote that, "God only spoke one Word [i.e. Jesus, the Word of God], and in that Word the whole creation came into being". Moreover, Fr Bede relates this understanding directly to St Paul's letter to the Ephesians (4:10): "He who descended is the very one who ascended higher than all the heavens, in order to fill the whole universe". Accordingly, Fr Bede accepts that the whole creation holds together in the Christ, the cosmic Person. In making this point he quotes Colossians 1:17 "He [Christ] is before all things, and in him all things hold together". At this point, as in others, Fr Bede's cosmic Christology was influenced significantly by the work of Pierre Teilhard de Chardin[7]. For Teilhard, Christ is seen to be the very centre of all creation. Teilhard writes in one of his early essays, 'Le Milieu mystique', as if it were Christ himself speaking:

> It is I [Christ] who am the true bond of the World. Without me, even if they appear to make contact with one another, beings are separated by an abyss. In me they meet, despite the Chaos of the age and of Space (Teilhard de Chardin in Lyons 1982:150).

Thus it must be reiterated again that for Fr Bede Christ has a universal and cosmic significance that is much broader than the Christian faith, its symbols and Church – this point will be discussed in more detail at a later stage (cf. Griffiths 1983:128).

Central to Fr Bede's desire was that Christians would see that God's salvific activity is not only for Christians but that it has significance for the whole cosmos. While the Church is a sacrament of Christ it does not contain him; rather the Church is to be a symbol, or sacrament, to the world of the true Christ who is its salvation. Fr Bede quotes the last verse of St Thomas Aquinas' hymn *Adore te devote latens deitas* in illustrating this. He writes:

> *Jesu quem velatum nunc aspicio, Oro fiat illud quod tam sitio, Ut te revelata cernens facie, Visu sims beatus tuae gloriae.* The translation, which really does not do justice to the beauty of the Latin, is: "Jesus whom I now see under a veil, grant that that may be which I so desire, that I may see Thee, face unveiled, and be blessed with the sight of Thy Glory". We pray that the veil may be taken away, the veil of the sacrament, so that the reality may appear.... Jesus, the humanity of Jesus, is a sacrament of God. It is a sign of God's grace, God's love, God's salvation, but we have to go beyond the sign to the reality (Griffiths 1983:129-130).

Lyons comments on Teilhard's cosmic Christology, with reference to this point, saying that:

> In Teilhard's view, Christ's Body is not merely mystical; that is, ecclesial. It is also cosmic, extending throughout the universe and comprising all things that attain their fulfilment in Christ. Fundamentally, the Body of Christ is the one single thing that is being made in creation (Lyons 1982:154-155).

Thus, Teilhard's cosmic Christology served to further enforce and develop Fr Bede's belief that Christ has a significance that is far greater than Christianity alone; Christ has a cosmic significance. Arising from his own Christology and influenced by Teilhard, Fr Bede concludes that the cosmic Christ is present in all forms of religion, including those general or cosmic forms of religion that predate Christianity (cf. Griffiths 1983:75; 1989:118-127 and Panikkar 1988:127-132). The following quote illustrates Fr Bede's position.

> It needs to be said that Christ is present in all religion. Jesus died for all humanity, without exception. So, from the beginning to the end of the world the grace of Christ through the cross is offered to every human being in some way, normally through their conscience, their traditions and customs or holy books (Griffiths 1992:96).

A more detailed discussion of the Fr Bede's theology of the cosmic Christ, and its ensuing implications for the Christian faith, will follow in chapters four and five. At this point it simply needs to be noted that Fr Bede found a great deal of resonance between his cosmic Christology and the highly developed notion of cosmic revelation evidenced in the Hindu scriptures generally, and the Upanishads in particular.

Thus, Fr Bede was aware of, and clearly accepted, a general or cosmic revelation that predated Christianity and has a broader significance than the Christian faith alone. However, he relates this general revelation specifically to the cosmic Christ, seeing it as a 'Christophony' and in this doctrine shows that Christ has a universal relevance for all religion, and all religions, but also a particular relevance for Christianity and the Christian church.

Particular or historical revelation

The second stage of revelation, as mentioned in the introduction to this chapter, is called historical or particular revelation. As its title suggests, it is based on a particular concept (or understanding) of time and a subsequent understanding of how God chooses to reveal God's self within that understanding of time and history.

The essential difference between historical and cosmic revelation relates to the historical view of time and the cosmic view of time. Wong points to the difference.

> The understanding of time in the Hindu and other Oriental cultures is cyclic. It rests on the rhythms of nature or the cosmic order with the endless recurrence of day and night and the four seasons of the year. In the Judeo-Christian tradition, however, time is linear. It has a beginning and is moving towards an end, an *eschaton*, with various *kairoi*, or moments of divine grace, in between (1996:2).

It is important to note the fundamental relationship between linear time and history within the Christian faith. In linear time history takes the form of events that follow one another chronologically. Thus, linear historical revelation conceives of God as revealing God's self not only in creation and the human soul, but also through the successive moments of human history in relation to people and the events that take place in their lives. For Christians, the incarnation of Jesus Christ forms the climax of God's gradual self-revelation in human history. In fact, Christianity derives from the historical event of Jesus Christ who was born at a particular time, in a particular place, lived for a certain span of time, and eventually died.

> This is what is specific in the Christian mystical experience. The absolute reality is experienced as revealed in Christ, in the life and death of Jesus of Nazareth. It is not an experience of absolute reality revealed in the Cosmos, in the cycle of time in nature, nor in the human Self, the psychic being with its capacity for self-transcendence, but in a historic person and a historic event (Griffiths 1982:179).

As a Christian Fr Bede emphasised the historical necessity of the incarnation of Jesus, a man of Nazareth, born in Bethlehem under a Roman Emperor, crucified by Pontius Pilate. This series of historical events illustrates a valuable part of the relationship between God and the created order (cf. Griffiths 1989:166-175). Wong notes that for Fr Bede this historical event

> ...reveals the unique character of the mystery of Incarnation. The real meaning of the Incarnation is that, by adopting our human nature, God fully enters into the world and history, sharing our human condition (1996:2).

In Fr Bede's own words:

> The ineffable Godhead, the one absolute reality, was revealed in the historic person of Jesus of Nazareth at a particular time in a particular place. It has to be emphasised that, in biblical faith, it is a matter of the infinite being manifest in the finite, the eternal in the temporal, in a specific time and place. This is a key point by which Christian revelation is distinguished from the Hindu and Buddhist view (1989:165).

The theological significance of this historic view of Christ will be discussed in chapter four. However, the essential aspect that needs to be noted at this stage is that while Fr Bede contrasts the cyclic and linear notions of time, he also suggests areas of complementarity between them.

The following serves as an example of this complementarity. A cyclic notion of time, such as that found in the philosophy that underpins Hinduism, tends to depreciate the meaning of events in this present world and its history. Fr Bede maintained that this view was, to a large extent, responsible for the situation of poverty in India. Christianity on the other hand, with its historical view, is very committed to the here and now, that is, to material and historical realities. At times Christians need reminding that the Kingdom of God cannot be solely identified with this present world. For this reason, Fr Bede says:

> The danger of Hinduism is that it tends to see time and history as a passing phenomenon without any ultimate significance. The danger of Christianity is that it tends to attach too much importance to temporal events and to lose the sense of timeless reality.... The Hindu surely needs to discover the real value of time and history.... But the Christian must learn that the Kingdom of God is not to be found in this world.... The Kingdom of God lies beyond history in the timeless reality in which all things find their fulfilment (Griffiths 1982:180-181).

However, it must also be noted that there are many Christians who maintain with vehemence that the Kingdom of God is not of this world and so do very little to change the world in which they live. A clear example of this is to be found in the Pentecostal and Charismatic Churches in South Africa and their lack of social awareness and involvement during the years of the apartheid struggle – this was aptly referred to as 'Church theology' in the Kairos document. The same criticism can be levelled against such Christians, as is levelled against the exclusively mystical expressions of the Hindu faith. I believe that Fr Bede's aim was not so to show that one needs a balance of two views of history. Rather, his aim was somewhat more pragmatic, emphasising that one needs a balance of perspective that takes both the present physical reality and the transcendent spiritual reality seriously.

Returning to Fr Bede's understanding of revelation, it is important to note at this point that his spirituality did not demand an acceptance of one form of revelation or truth over another. Rather, Fr Bede's desire was for truth, regardless of where it came from. Consequently he was able to integrate both cosmic and particular revelation into the expression of his cosmic Christology, in such a way that they were complementary of one another.

Fr Bede's understanding of revelation, as taking place in both cosmic and historical forms, is an essential aspect that informs and shapes his theology of the cosmic Christ. The Hindu, cyclic view of time serves as a corrective for some Christians who place an overemphasis on the historical Christ, while the Christian view of time and history is able to emphasise the fact that God, in Christ, is active in human and cosmic history.

Three levels of reality

A further essential aspect to understanding Fr Bede's theology of the cosmic Christ is his view of reality, i.e., his cosmology. In accordance with the standard Hindu view of the cosmos, he maintained that the universe is made up of three interdependent and interconnected aspects of reality, namely the physical, the psychological and the spiritual (1982:184). Fr Bede observes that this view of reality was the commonly accepted view of the ancient world, but that it had been lost in contemporary western society and culture. However, as he pointed out, this view is regaining acceptance amongst those who accept the new science (cf. Griffiths 1982:183; 1983:20 and the following section for a more detailed discussion on the elements of the new science that Fr Bede used in his theology).

Fr Bede maintained that the generally accepted western understanding of the world, based on Cartesian philosophy and Newtonian physics, is limited since it attempts to explain all of reality in mechanistic and reductionist terms. He noted that if one subscribed only to this materialist view of the cosmos one's view of reality would not only be limited in scope but also fundamentally wrong (1989:15). This limited view of reality imposes a radical subject/object distinction by maintaining that matter is merely an "extended substance" that is extended outside of the human mind (Griffiths referring to Descartes 1983:20). Fr Bede summarises his understanding of this limited viewpoint as follows. In this dualistic viewpoint

> ...we have a mind, and that mind is quite different and distinct from this matter, this world. Science is the process of the mind observing this external world. Then, for those who believe in religion, beyond this matter and

> beyond this mind there is a God, above everything. That
> is the three-tiered universe which we have inherited
> (1983:20).

Fr Bede's own view of reality differs significantly from this understanding. In formulating his view of reality Fr Bede integrated elements of the new science with those of perennial philosophy and eastern religion. In particular he aligned himself with an understanding of reality that no longer conceived of matter as 'extended substance' (to use Descartes term), but rather as a web of interconnected relations that form an organic whole[8]. Such a view of reality would not be entirely foreign to the eastern mind. However, for western culture and religion with its strong emphasis on rugged individualism it is somewhat strange. Drawing on scientific views such as the one that was made popular by scientists such David Bohm and philosophers of science such as Fritjof Capra, Fr Bede was given a suitable vocabulary for sharing his experiences of a cosmos that is fundamentally united in Christ with the westerners who visited the ashram.

Fr Bede also maintained, as an extension of this basic non-dual view of the cosmos, that the physical world could not be separated from the human psyche, which he referred to as "the consciousness" (1983:20).

> Instead of a separate, extended world and separate mind
> we have a field of energy which has its own laws and
> structures but which is also interdependent with the
> whole   psychological   world,   the   world   of
> consciousness.... You cannot separate the world from
> consciousness any more (Griffiths 1983:20).

Beyond the physical and psychic 'worlds', Fr Bede maintained that there is the spiritual world which "though separate from matter and soul is yet interwoven in the whole structure" of the cosmos (1983:20). Of course this view the cosmos is not alien to Christianity; in fact it can be found in the theology of St Paul, the Church Fathers, Irenaeus and Origen. For Fr Bede the resurrection of Jesus Christ is a sign of this integral reality.

> His physical body did not disintegrate, but was reunited
> with his soul, his psyche. Soul and body did not

'disappear' but were transfigured by the indwelling
Spirit (Griffiths 1984:184).

Fr Bede's cosmic Christology draws a great deal of inspiration from
this non-dual view of reality. He found a great deal of resonance
between his mystical experience of this cosmic unity and the
postulations of the new physics that interprets the universe in an
interdependent and organic manner. In relation to the cosmic Christ,
the resurrection of Jesus Christ is thus a sign of the new creation, and
also its actual inauguration. Such an assertion is based on the
understanding that since the body of Christ is part of the one cosmos,
which is a continuum or interrelated system, his resurrection has
consequences for the whole of reality. The resurrection life that
permeates the resurrected body of Christ permeates all of creation,
since his body and the rest of creation are fundamentally one. Wong
emphasizes Fr Bede's understanding of the resurrection of Christ in
relation to this point as follows:

> Through the instrumentality of the glorified Christ, the
> Spirit took possession of matter and the entire creation,
> initiating the process of transmutation of the cosmos into
> a new creation (1996:5).

Thus, Fr Bede's cosmic Christology is intrinsically linked to his view
of the universe as a single interlinked and independent whole. A more
in-depth and technical discussion of the science, philosophy and
psychology (that form the framework through which Fr Bede
expressed his views) will take place in the section, 'A new vision of
reality', that follows next.

A new vision of reality

As stated above, Fr Bede viewed the universe as consisting of three
interdependent and interrelated dimensions, namely the physical, the
psychological, and the spiritual (Griffiths 1989:278). These also
happen to be the generally accepted categories of ontological reality
within the Hindu philosophical and religious framework. However,
what makes Fr Bede's spirituality so novel and appealing is that he not
only drew on Hinduism to substantiate and explain his view of reality
(thereby making his views acceptable to the eastern mind); he also
makes use of the predominant expression of the West, namely science,
to get his point across to the western mindset. Many, including myself,

have found this to be a very attractive and appealing element in his spirituality. Through marrying elements of eastern mysticism with aspects of the new science in the west he is able to appeal to a much broader spectrum of spiritual seeker. It is true that Fr Bede only drew selectively on elements of eastern mysticism and western science in articulating his marriage of East and West, however, the same could be said of any spirituality or articulation of spirituality. In spite of this selectivity, Fr Bede's spirituality results in a more balanced approach to reality than either a purely eastern or western spiritual perspective (each having their own deficiencies and biases in turn). His spirituality thus showed how insights and developments in the new science relate to the three categories of reality that have long been held and accepted in eastern mysticism.

This section will discuss this specific complementarity between science and mysticism in Fr Bede's worldview. In doing this, an outline of Fr Bede's views of science, biology, psychology and the perennial philosophy will be given. For more detail on each of these subjects it would be necessary for the more serious scholar to read Fr Bede's own works (references to these can be found in the select bibliography at the end of this book). Accordingly, the insights gained from this discussion will serve as valuable window into Fr Bede's, approach to, and understanding of, the cosmic Christ.

Fr Bede believed that the world was on the verge of a 'new age' (Griffiths 1989:9). This emerging epoch, or new age, would come as a result of two things: first, it would come as a result of a collapse of the current, inadequate, world-view (Griffiths 1989:295). Second, it would come as a result of a 'new vision of reality' stemming from credible and substantial discoveries in a variety of spheres and disciplines. He believed that a new view of the cosmos, humanity, creation, and spirituality in the areas of science, biology, psychology and religion would more widely accepted, the sense of the sacred would return and come to pervade all levels of society.

As was briefly mentioned above, Fr Bede felt that the largely accepted Newtonian/Cartesian view of reality was inadequate to address the complexity of reality that is more than just physically (i.e., a reality that is physical, spiritual and psychological in nature) (1989:9). His optimism in this new worldview was fuelled by developments in western thought over the last hundred years, and particularly the later half of the twentieth century. He believed that the inadequate materialist view of reality was being undermined and challenged by developments in science in particular, but also in psychology and spirituality.

The sections below will give an overview some of these understandings and developments from science, psychology, and religion. These points will then be related to the positive contribution Fr Bede believed they could make to a variety of disciplines and fields of study.

Science

The materialist philosophy that has pervaded our society has its roots, as outlined above, in a worldview that asserts that material reality is primary, and that all of the universe simply functions as a complex mechanism. The most significant influence on this worldview comes from the work of the enlightenment philosopher, Rene Descartes. His philosophy in turn is strongly influenced by Aristotelian philosophy with its belief that all human knowledge is based upon evidence received from the senses (touch, taste, hearing, smell and sight). Many of us would not question this supposition. However, if one maintains that *all* knowledge (and thus all truth) is fundamentally discovered through one's senses, it leaves very little space for either God's revelation, or the place of spiritual discovery. Descartes took this materialist view of reality further than previous philosophers in being the first person to assert that there is a complete separation between 'mind' and 'matter'. Aristotle had maintained that the human person is a body-soul, the soul is the form of the human body. Thus, in the Aristotelian view the person remains an integrated whole (cf. Griffiths 1989:12). Descartes, on the other hand, held that all matter, including the human body, is extended outside of the mind, that is, separate from the 'person' i.e., completely separate from the mind. There is a radical subject/object distinction between 'the mind' and 'the world'. Essentially the mind looks out on the universe as it extends outside of the person.

Following along these lines it would be possible for a person to objectively study all things outside of him or her self. Descartes, as a mathematician, believed that through mathematical calculation one could come to a perfect understanding of the universe. For him the universe was merely a complex mechanism, governed by mathematical laws and principles which, once discovered, could explain all reality.

This view maintains that each person is a separated, self-contained, thinking reality (*res cogitans*) over against the material reality (*res extensa*) of the rest of the universe (cf. Griffiths 1989:13). A further development, in relation to the materialist worldview, came from Francis Bacon, the English philosopher. He said that the goal of science was not only to understand the universe (i.e., to objectively study and quantify it), but to control it by applying the principles discovered in scientific and empirical investigation. Galileo made the next important contribution to this world-view by adding that mass and motion were the main characteristics of matter. Thus, since mass and motion are measurable, all matter could be measured quantitatively. The *res extensa* (material reality) is thus quantitative, allowing it to be measured and studied objectively. Aspects of reality such as faith, beauty and emotions began to be regarded as subjective and of no scientific value. Since this view held that they had no scientific value they began to have less value generally in western society, which was largely regulated by mechanistic and reductionist principles.

The next major contribution to this world-view was that of Isaac Newton, the Cambridge physicist, whose metaphysical model of the universe still dominates much of contemporary science to date. Newton said that reality could be explained in terms of a number of laws (especially concerning mass and motion), such as his famous law of gravity. These laws, he contended, governed all of creation. For Newton all reality consisted of concrete objects moving in space and time. Fr Bede comments on the significance of this saying,

> Measurement of mass, motion and other properties, and their interrelationships, provided the model of the universe for the succeeding centuries ... the method of Newtonian mechanics was so highly successful and yielded such impressive results it became extrapolated into metaphysics. It was assumed that philosophically Newtonian physics provided not only a complete picture of reality but the only picture of reality (1989:14-15).

The result of this world-view has very often led to the exclusion of anything that was not objectively quantifiable, and scientifically capable of manipulation and control, from the sphere of highest concern for humanity. It is from this purely mechanistic understanding of creation that the dominant materialistic approach to reality comes. In its most extreme form there is no longer a need for belief in God since all of creation is seen to be regulated by laws and principles that are purely mathematical. Moreover, it has often been maintained that if a person could discover these laws, and then learn how to manipulate them, that person could ensure the smooth running of nature, and the contentment of human persons. In a general sense this is often regarded as a common view amongst groups such as the Marxists. However, in less stringent forms this world-view can be seen to permeate almost all of western society in subtle ways.

Such a view of reality is clearly inadequate. In the West it is becoming increasingly obvious that the concept of a mechanism is far too simplistic to describe the complexity of the whole of reality. Fritjof Capra's book *The Tao of Physics* (1975) has been significant in spreading awareness of this. Recent discoveries in quantum physics have shown that the material universe is not so much a mechanism as "a field of energies in which the parts can only be understood in relation to the whole" (Griffiths 1989:17). Thus, the universe is more accurately likened to an organic, living entity (like a cell), rather than a mechanistic system (like a clock).

For Fr Bede, David Bohm's theory of implicate and explicate orders gives a much more complete, and credible, reflection of reality (and even physical reality) than the Cartesian/Newtonian model (Griffiths 1989:18). Bohm's view is that all material reality is an explication of a vast number of implicate orders. He maintains that underlying the explicate order there is a "deeper order of existence, a vast and more primary level of reality that gives birth to all objects and appearances of our physical world" (Talbot 1991:46). Hence this world-view would hold that what we perceive as physical reality is not a number of separate self-contained objects (as in the Cartesian/Newtonian world-view) but rather, reality is a dynamic whole, an explication of the undivided whole that is in a perpetual state of flux[9] (Bohm 1980:185).

What Fr Bede found so significant in this view of reality is its emphasis on the unity and interconnectivity of created reality. There is in this view, a sense of non-duality - all reality is ultimately one,

> ... behind the explicate order the implicate is always
> present, so in that sense the whole universe is implicated
> behind every explicit form (Griffiths 1989:18).

This notion of the implicate and explicate orders is also referred to as the 'holomovement' by Bohm (Keepin 1993:34). Bohm explains that the structure of reality can be likened to a holographic image. In holography a photographic record is not two a dimensional record of an object as in traditional photography. Rather, a holograph is a set of interference patterns made by splitting a laser beam and reflecting some of the beam off the object itself, before reuniting it with the rest of the beam on the photographic plate. The plate captures a three dimensional image. When a laser beam is directed onto the photographic plate the three-dimensional image of the object appears. What makes this analogy more remarkable to an interconnected, spirit permeated, worldview is that if the laser beam is directed on only a small part of the holograph the entire image still appears, although less distinctly (Keepin 1993:34). In an analogous manner holography suggests how all of (explicate) creation is a manifestation of an ever-changing, single, (implicate) reality. A further element to the analogy of implicate and explicate orders comes from the understanding of reality being in flux. The explicate order is constantly in a state of change since it continually comes out of, and moves back into, the implicate order. The resulting assertion of the above is thus a theory that suggests that each part of creation contains within it the whole (the whole is made up of the parts, yet the parts contain the whole – they are mutually interdependent, interpenetrating and enlivening one another).

Theologically this is significant, as it implies that we are living in a universe that is not separate from ourselves (or more particularly, separate from 'self'). We ourselves are the universe, this universe is us. We are an explication of the one ultimate reality. There is a fundamental sense of interconnectedness between all persons and all of creation. We are one, one with the Creator, all creation and of course also ourselves. Fr Bede related this idea to Ken Wilber's early work on the 'spectrum of consciousness', where at the deepest levels of consciousness a person becomes aware of being one with all reality (cf. Wilber 1975)[10]. Wilber's model will be discussed in greater detail in below. What Fr Bede found so noteworthy in this view, in relation to his cosmic Christology, is that it affirms cosmic unity at a deep level (implicate), yet at the same time it also affirms differentiation. As Teilhard de Chardin said, "Unity differentiates"[11] (cf. Lyons 1982:165). In the explicate order there are different manifestations or explications of the one implicate reality. As a person I am an explication (an individual) of the implicate (collective) reality. While Fr Bede never used Beatrice Bruteau's understanding of identity, there is a great deal of resonance between Fr Bede's use of the implicate and explicate orders in showing how unity differentiates, and Bruteau's view. She says that identity no longer depends on negation of the rest of creation. A person is not an individual or differentiated from the rest of creation, in saying "I am I insofar as I am not you" (Bruteau 1990:128). Rather, differentiation comes from the implicate order. Our individuality comes from the One, the Source, the Ultimate Reality in, and behind, all creation. In this new view of reality a person could say, "I am I in so far as I am in you and you are in me". Of course Wilber's later work on 'holons' would also speak strongly in favour of Fr Bede's views. For example a book contains a rich and diverse unified message. However, the book is nothing without the sentences that make up the message. Yet at the same time the sentences are nothing without the words, and the words are meaningless without the individual letters that form their constitutive parts. So, in this sense, each part is simultaneously a part and a whole, implicate and explicate. Moreover, no one part is more or less important than the other. The letters are dependent on the higher levels for their meaning, but the book is dependent upon the letters for its meaning (I have discussed this elsewhere, see Forster 2006, chapter four, but particularly 2006:175-184).

Fr Bede, Beatrice Bruteau, and Wilber's views offer a radically different perspective from the Cartesian/Newtonian view of reality in that they affirm that there is an ontological interdependence and interconnectivity between all of reality, and all of material reality is pervaded by, and finds its true explanation in, the transcendent reality (Griffiths 1989:11). Fr Bede affirmed this as a positive development, in that the mechanistic model of reality is being replaced with a living or organic model (1989:278)[12].

One must, however, not think that Fr Bede did not value, or appreciate, the Cartesian/Newtonian worldview – quite the opposite. He affirmed that this worldview had contributed a great deal to knowledge, science, and even human development. He does grant that a high view of material reality is valuable in so far as it recognises the material basis of reality, and that science within that model has made great advances through exploring a material view of reality (1989:278-279). Fr Bede even uses the word "correct" in reference to materialism, his intention is not to suggest that it is entirely correct, however, since he refers to the numerous flaws of this view on many occasions (cf. 1982:9). Rather, his suggestion is that materialism is correct only in so far as it recognises "the material basis of reality, and science has explored this basis further than has ever been done before" (1989:278-279). Here one can again see the integrative and transcendent aspect of Fr Bede's spirituality. He affirms that which is of value in materialist science, but also points out that one needs to move beyond it in order to move closer to the truth of reality. Consequently he goes on to say that this age, dominated by individualism, science and capitalism, is flawed in that it has lost sight of the sacred within and behind the material world (1989:279). Once again what Fr Bede advocates, as was seen in the section on cosmic and historical revelation (see chapter three), is a balance that recognises both material and spiritual reality.

Biology

One of the consequences of the reductionist and mechanistic views of reality has been an attempt to explain life in terms of physics and chemistry alone (Griffiths 1989:20). Fr Bede sought to affirm developments in the biological sciences, yet, as with the physical sciences, he sought out scholarly work that would attest to the spiritual, implicate, reality at work within and around all matter. He found such a notion in the work of the biologist, Rupert Sheldrake. Fr Bede agrees with Rupert Sheldrake that even though molecular biology has made some pertinent discoveries, it is not comprehensive enough to explain the main features of life in their complexity and entirety. This inadequacy becomes particularly apparent in relation to the process of morphogenesis, that is, the development of new forms of life, and their regulation and regeneration, in relation to morphogenetic fields (1989:20). Therefore, Fr Bede notes that Sheldrake has made a significant contribution to the new vision of reality with the introduction of the notion of 'formative causation' or morphogenesis (1989:20).

The theory that has been dominant in the biological sciences in contemporary academic research can best be described as a form of neo-Darwinianism. Broadly, it asserts that the evolutionary development of organisms can be accounted for in terms of random mutations, Mendelian genetics, and processes of natural selection. Fr Bede, following Sheldrake, questions this neo-Darwinian view. His aim is to argue in favour of returning to a view that recognises the presence of God in creation (both as creator and sustainor). He does this by drawing upon the principles of complexity that are found in material objects. First, he questions how random mutation can account completely for the complex process of electrons and protons being organised to form atoms, which in turn form molecules, and ultimately how the organisation of molecules can form cells which become plants and even more highly developed self conscious life forms, such as human persons. Sheldrake, as a biologist, puts forward the hypothesis that although the universe is made up of fields of energy, these fields of energy cannot explain the complexity of a living Universe entirely. Thus, in conjunction with these fields of energy, there must be some formative cause or power. It is these fields or powers that Sheldrake calls morphogenetic fields.

> The Greek word *morphē* means form, hence 'morphogenetic' is that which produces forms. (Griffiths 1989:20).

Morphogenetic fields, also referred to as morphic fields, can be likened to the Aristotelian notion of soul or 'entelechies' that give form to substance (Sheldrake 1996:350). From this assumption Sheldrake moves on to suggest that the universe, as it is, is constructed not only of matter, but also of 'form'. Matter is potential energy; it has no existence of itself. Matter only has the potential to exist. Sheldrake's assertion is that matter is structured in the universe by form, what Aristotle would have called *eidos* (also meaning shape or form). Sheldrake suggests something similar to Aristotle, in saying that matter is being organised by morphogenetic fields (Sheldrake 1996:350). An animal is an animal because it is matter that is organised within a particular morphogenetic field, while at the same time it is also in resonance with other similar organisms. So the universe, in this view, can be seen as developing through two forces working together. First, there is energy or matter that has no structure. Second, there is form, or the morphogenetic fields, that give structure to the matter of the universe.

Form + matter

Recapturing the essential argument of this view was of seminal theological importance to Fr Bede, since it suggested that all of creation is dependent on the order or form of the cosmos for its meaning and structure. Sheldrake says that, "[b]odies of all kinds derive their physical activity and material existence from the flowing energy within them... they are pervaded by spirit..." (1996:353).

Fr Bede agrees with Sheldrake's hypothesis on form and matter in saying that,

> The whole creation, from the smallest atom to the furthest star, is a manifestation in space and time, in multiplicity and change, of that unchanging One.... From the first beginning of matter, through all the stages of evolution, of organic growth and consciousness, the Spirit is structuring these forms, moulding them by her inherent power (1982:193).

A view such as this goes a long way towards restoring an awareness of the sacred within the cosmos. For Fr Bede the cosmic Person is the source and form, as well as the sustainer, of all creation. A discussion on the significance of a rediscovery of the sacredness of creation will take place in chapter five.

Psychology

A third aspect of importance within this new paradigm relates to the implications that it has for the understanding of the human psyche. Within the schema of Fr Bede's new vision of reality, the clearest connection between science and psychology comes from the work of Teilhard de Chardin (cf. Griffiths 1989:25). Teilhard's view shows a connection between the evolution of consciousness and the evolution of the cosmos[13]. In discussing this connection he uses metaphorical language to describe material reality. He speaks of two forces that operate within creation. They are the radial and the tangential forces. Teilhard suggests that there is a centre out of which the whole world moves. At every moment of time there is, as it were, a sphere and the particles on that sphere are governed by a tangential force that corresponds to forces spoken of in physics, such as gravity and electromagnetism. The tangential forces are forces that organise order in matter. Along with this there is also a radial force that encourages an evolutionary outward movement to higher levels of reality. The radial force, according to Teilhard, is 'spirit' and he speaks of it in terms of Christ-consciousness (Griffiths 1989:26). The point towards which all of the cosmos is evolving in consciousness is the "Christ-Omega" (de Chardin 1965:167). Lyons comments on Teilhard's evolutionary view saying that:

> Creation, incarnation, and redemption constitute the one movement, which Teilhard calls 'pleromization'. It is a movement towards the 'pleroma', the fullness of being, in which God and his completed world exist united together (Lyons 1982:156).

Thus, as the universe matures, the strength of this radial force increases in intensity. Hence the universe is constantly emerging into consciousness as it evolves. Fr Bede recognised this understanding of an evolution of consciousness in the universe as a significant link between science and psychology within the ambit of his view of reality (Griffiths 1989:26). The present state of human consciousness is relatively rudimentary, but there is an increasing discovery that human consciousness can develop beyond its current level to a level that Teilhard calls 'hypermental', and Sri Aurobindo[14] calls the 'supramental' consciousness, that is, a level of consciousness and experience that is beyond the personal and mental. Fr Bede describes such consciousness as transpersonal and transmental (Griffiths 1989:27). He says that at this level of consciousness we discover within ourselves "the ground of the whole structure of the universe and the whole scope of human consciousness" (1989:27).

This is a psychological breakthrough beyond mere 'mental' consciousness to the 'supramental'; it is a discovery of the ground of all creation, that Ultimate Reality that sustains the whole universe. This level, and realisation, of consciousness is not a new discovery. As is suggested in chapter three, such forms of consciousness predate Christianity and can be evidenced in those early religions that are identified with cosmic revelation. Fr Bede records examples of how early Indian philosophers in the Vedas referred to rita (ṛta) as the cosmic order that underlies the whole of the universe. This led them to see the ground of all existence in Brahman and the ground of all consciousness in the Atman, the inner self (Griffiths 1995:x). Fr Bede notes with interest that there was a similar experience, referred to as nirvana, that took place in Buddhism at roughly the same time in history.

evolution of universe

=

evolution of consciousness

> Gautama Siddhartha, the Buddha, piercing through the outer worlds of the senses, which is always subject to change and decay, was able to experience the transcendent mystery of *nirvana*... the passing away of all phenomena and the awareness of the void (*sunyata*), that which remains when all images and concepts have been surpassed and the mind dwells in the silent depths of its original being (Griffiths 1995:xi).

Experiences such as these, of which there are numerous examples in various cultures and religions, give strong credence to the notion of a cosmic revelation. In effect the assertion is that the same cosmic Lord that is revealed in all of nature is the cosmic Lord that is revealed within the human soul. Fr Bede's approach was to utilise multiple disciplines in articulating his world-view, since these disciplines show a correlation between his understanding of interconnectivity in the cosmos as expressed in science, and in this psychological view of consciousness. The common ground articulated in both of these disciplines is that the whole universe is in each of us, implicated in a multitude of complexifying layers. This united state of the whole cosmos is thus not only a physical reality, but also a psychological and spiritual reality.

As stated earlier, there is a psychological distinction between the self and creation within the mechanistic and reductionist world-view. Hence, we tend to think of the rest of the universe as outside of and apart from ourselves. The new science however suggests a vastly different reality. Karl Pribram, a friend of David Bohm, was the first to use an understanding of holography as a metaphor for reality (see chapter three for a discussion on David Bohm's use of holography in relation to his quantum theory). Pribram related holography to psychology. His suggestion is that we receive vibrations of light, sound and matter into our brains and then, as in the case of the hologram, we project a three-dimensional image of the world around ourselves (Griffiths 1989:31). This does not mean that the world does not exist. The energy is real and it is this energy that projects on our brains. Rather, what is suggested in this hypothesis is that the way in which we perceive the world depends largely upon our level of consciousness. A greater consciousness will lead to far truer perception of reality. Jung was the first psychologist to propose something similar to this when he referred to the collective unconscious. Fr Bede mentions Jung's view in saying,

the way we perceive the world depends on our level of consciousness.

> We have inherited from the past archetypes which are
> structured forms or patterns of organic energy, in which
> the unconscious reflects its experiences (Griffiths
> 1989:32).

As has been pointed out, Fr Bede was particularly fascinated by the
work of Ken Wilber and his explanation of consciousness. Wilber's
notion is that human consciousness is a multi-levelled manifestation, or
expression, of a single Consciousness, just as in physics the electro-
magnetic spectrum is a multi-banded wave (Wilber 1975:106) [15]. Thus
as conscious beings we are manifestations of the one Ultimate Reality
at different levels, depending on which level we identify with on the
'spectrum of consciousness'. The spectrum ranges from identity with
God, others, self and the world – going through several gradations or
bands to the drastically narrowed sense of identity referred to as egoic
consciousness (Wilber 1975:106). At the deepest level the person's
consciousness is identical with the Absolute and Ultimate Reality of
the universe, known variously as brahman or tao or the Godhead.

> On this level, man is identified with the universe, the All
> - or rather, he *is* the All.... In short, man's innermost
> consciousness... is identical to the ultimate reality of the
> universe. (Wilber 1975:107-108).

Such an understanding of consciousness was used by Fr Bede to show
that cosmic unity is more than just physical or biological and that
essentially all of creation is interconnected at every level. Relating the
above view to the scientific hypothesis of David Bohm, it can be said
that we are all explications of the one implicate reality, interconnected
with all creation and with God. However, the way in which people
perceive this unity depends on their state, or level, of consciousness.
All creation is always one – that is an ontological reality. However,
some aspects may seem separated from the self because one's
conscious development may be at a lower level on the spectrum of
consciousness. An example of this would be a person that is on the
existential level. Here the person makes a distinction between self and
environment. One sees all creation as outside of, and separate from,
who one believes one is. Thus such a person's state of consciousness is
a consciousness of distinction and separation; it is the way in which he
or she will perceive him or herself in relation to creation.

While Ken Wilber's own theories have evolved since Fr Bede's
death, the discussion above serves to give some indication as to what

role Fr Bede saw the human psyche taking within his view of the cosmos. This discussion is of significance in understanding Fr Bede's theology of the cosmos, in that it clearly displays his view that all creation is united to (not separate from) its Creator. All persons can know that they are one with God, one with the rest of the world, and one with others and Self. Through meditation and other spiritual disciplines the individual can reach a level of Supreme Identity. I have often faced criticism when speaking to contemporary Christians about this view. Somehow an assumption, or perhaps a perversion, of dualism has crept into contemporary spirituality and theology that assumes radical separation from God and the rest of God's creation, rather than true unity with God and all that God creates and sustains. In fact, we need to be reminded that the Protestant tradition affirms the fact that we are *simul justus et peccator*, that is, at once justified, one with God, creation and self, yet through our sin we cut ourselves off from that supreme consciousness and we experience reality at a lower level.

Thus, non-dual consciousness within the cosmos is a central theme in Fr Bede's psychology of the 'new vision of reality'. At the level of supreme identity non-duality is an essential element in Fr Bede's spirituality. However, Fr Bede recognised that some level of duality is present, and even necessary, at lower levels of consciousness in order for the cosmos and society to function (e.g. to be able to differentiate different persons and places as unique and different is a necessary duality for the functioning of society – yet it is a functional reality, rather than an ontological reality).

The perennial philosophy

The next important element that shapes Fr Bede's cosmic Christology is what is referred to as 'the perennial philosophy'[16]. Until the sixteenth century there was a universal philosophy throughout the civilised world that was known as the "perennial philosophy" (Griffiths 1989:10). According to Fr Bede (1989:11) this universal wisdom prevailed from about 500 A.D. until about 1500 A.D.

This philosophy was based on the belief that all of the cosmos is pervaded by, and could find its explanation in, a transcendent reality. Whilst this claim may not sound strange to readers of this book, one simply needs to consider that the largely secular West, and the paradigms of secular science and self sufficiency have caused this view to be questioned by many educated and thinking people. Gradually however, as shown in the discussion about the materialistic worldview in chapter three above, a mechanistic and materialistic view of reality began to take dominance over the 'sacred' view. Sadly this eventually led to the eradication of the perennial philosophy in most western societies (Griffiths 1989:11). Whilst I say that this eradication took place mainly in the West, the forces of secularism and materialism can also be evidenced in those cultures and societies where western thought was adopted. To a large extent, though, the perennial philosophy was maintained in the cultures of the East.

The psychologist, Stanislav Grof, suggests that the reason for this retention of the sacred in the East is that the eastern mind-set is far more open to a cosmic consciousness and creative intelligence as primary attributes of existence (Grof 1984:4). The advantages of this view of reality are numerous. For instance, whereas the materialistic view of reality sees humans as highly developed animals or thinking biological machines, the perennialist view see humans as one with the whole universe and its transcendent creator; humans are regarded as essentially divine, or at very least fundamentally in touch with the divine (Grof 1984:4). Materialistic science is reductionist, seeking to alleviate human suffering by sociological and psychopharmacological means. The perennial philosophy, on the other hand, is far more spiritual, seeking to liberate the spirit of the person. Fr Bede did affirm that western science and materialism had done much to alleviate physical suffering, but sadly they had neglected genuine spiritual and emotional fulfilment in the process (1989:279). He remarked that cultures such as those of the East, that have maintained the perennial philosophy, have had a much stronger emphasis on spiritual liberation (Griffiths 1989:279). However, their struggle, in turn, was that they often failed to offer practical solutions for the problems of everyday existence. Fr Bede's suggestion was that there needs to be a combination of the positive aspects of the perennial philosophy with the positive aspects of western science in order to have a holistic existence, meeting the needs of body, mind and spirit (Griffiths 1989:281). This is what Fr Bede meant when he spoke of the marriage of East and West.

Once again, one is able to observe some characteristic elements of Fr Bede's spirituality emerging from this discussion. First, there is his emphasis on recapturing the sense of the sacred in creation. Second, one is able to identify his desire to see a marriage between the positive aspects in eastern and in western culture that would move human consciousness to a higher level of truth, a truth that transcends any one cultural or religious approach to the complexity of reality.

Conclusion

This section of the book has given an overview of the philosophical and theological background from which Fr Bede developed his cosmic Christology. It has shown that Fr Bede drew upon a number of disciplines in order to understand and express his experience of reality as sacred and interconnected. It is important to remember that Fr Bede draws upon the insights of these concepts and philosophies, not because he believes they are fully able to express the truth of the cosmic Christ that he has experienced, but rather because they are able to give further insight, a new vocabulary, and helpful conceptual expressions to his spiritual experience. However, at the end of the day, even though these vehicles are helpful to take one closer to the truth, they will also need to be abandoned once their symbolic meaning comes to an end.

All of the areas discussed above have gone through significant changes since Fr Bede's death. I am certain that he would have found the subsequent theories and discoveries stimulating and challenging, and would have been critical about incorporating and interpreting such developments. However, the discussion above is sufficient to illustrate Fr Bede's use of, and reliance upon, multiple disciplines in conveying his spirituality.

Having laid the groundwork, the next chapter will discuss aspects of Fr Bede's theology of the cosmic Christ.

Chapter 4

Between two horizons: Aspects of the cosmic Christ in the spirituality of Bede Griffiths

> For the salvation of those who are good, for the destruction of evil in man, for the fulfilment of the kingdom of righteousness, I come to this world in ages that pass (<u>Bhagavad Gita</u> quoted in Griffiths 1987:66).

This quotation is taken from the Bhagavad Gita, referring to the Hindu concept of incarnation where an *avatara* (a descent of God into the world) enters creation for the salvation of the world (cf. Griffiths 1987:66). In this regard one can see that, on some level at least, Christianity and Hinduism both place similar emphases on God's desire to save the world, and the importance of God becoming 'incarnate', entering into the created world, in order to achieve this goal. Naturally, for the Hindu and the Christian, investigating such similarities can be mutually enriching, offering a broader understanding of the mystery of God in creation. However, such an investigation must be entered into with a measure of discernment, as shall be discussed later on, since even though some of the concepts and language may relate between Hinduism and Christianity, there are still radical theological and philosophical differences between these two important faiths.

Hence, this section of the book intends to examine aspects of Fr Bede's cosmic Christology in greater theological detail. Please don't be deterred by the thought of having to consider complex theological and philosophical concepts! Most of what is discussed below is done in an accessible manner.

Thus, the discussion will point out areas in which Fr Bede draws on Hindu theology in order to enrich his understanding and expression of his Christology, and vice versa. Since one cannot directly transfer Hindu and Christian theologies into each other without encountering considerable philosophical and conceptual difficulty, there will also be a focus on areas of divergence between Fr Bede's cosmic Christology and understandings of the cosmic Person and incarnation that are found in Hinduism. Another important area, that requires further theological investigation in addition to the discussion in the previous chapter, is Fr Bede's understanding of the relationship between the cosmic Christ and created order.

Thus, this section of the book will examine how and why Fr Bede chooses to use the language and concepts of Hinduism to express and articulate his experience of the person and work of Christ. In addition to this there will be some discussion of how Fr Bede views the differences between the person of Christ and incarnations in other religious traditions (particularly Hinduism). To start with it is necessary to gain some insight into Fr Bede's approach to, and understanding of, the doctrine of the cosmic Christ as it has developed within Christianity.

An examination of the manner in which Fr Bede understands and utilises traditional cosmic Christology.

Cosmic Christology has a long and rich history in the Christian tradition – it is certainly not new to mainstream Christology, neither is it foreign to those theologians who are located primarily within the ambit of orthodox Christian theology. Before pointing out some of the significant ways in which the doctrine developed, it is useful to briefly examine the meaning of the term 'cosmic Christ'.

Within Christian doctrine this term is used to refer to a particular understanding of the person and work of Jesus Christ. The adjective 'cosmic' is derived from the Greek word κόσμος, which refers to the whole of the universe or created order. As will be seen below, the notion of the cosmic Christ is used to explain the manner in which Christ is related to the whole of the created order. A further emphasis in cosmic Christology is that Christ's relationship with the created order stretches beyond human and earthly affairs. By this it is meant that the cosmic Christ has a broader significance than the historical view of the person of Jesus of Nazareth, a view that often confines his significance to one period of history (even if that is the whole of human history), and often to one geographical location. The doctrine of the cosmic

Christ has significance that stretches beyond one particular culture or religion or planet. In essence the doctrine of the cosmic Christ affirms that Christ has significance for the whole of the cosmos or created order and not just for the Christian faith and those human persons who adhere to it. The cosmic Christ has significance for animals, for plants, and even for inanimate objects such as planets and stars.

The essential elements of this doctrine have developed over a long period of time and continue to do so today as new developments in a variety of disciplines interpret the significance of Christ for the cosmos. The doctrine of the cosmic Christ, in its earliest Christian form, can be traced back to the New Testament. The Epistles, and particularly the writings of St Paul, contribute towards our understanding of, and bear testimony to, the development of this aspect of the doctrine of Christ (cf. Colossians 1:15-18; Ephesians 1:10)[17].

The Church Fathers further developed the New Testament understanding of the cosmic significance of Christ, and ingrained these ideas into subsequent Christian doctrine. One of the earliest explicit articulations of cosmic Christology amongst the Church Fathers comes from Origen (c.185 – c. 254 AD) who writes, in reference to Revelation 22:13, that

> ... God the Logos is the Alpha, the beginning and the cause of all things, the one who is first not in time but in honour.... Let it be said that, since he provides an end for the thing created from him, he is the Omega at the consummation of the ages. He is first and then he is last, not in relation to time, but because he provides beginning and end (Origen quoted in Lyons 1982:130-131).

Thus, in Origen there is already a clear understanding of all of creation having Christ as its source and goal. Christ is the one who 'recapitulates' all of creation within himself. Gregory of Nazianzus (d. 389 AD) also expressed an understanding of Christ as being present in the whole of the cosmos. He writes succinctly that, "Christ exists in all things that are" (in Fox 1988:75). The doctrine further developed in mainstream theology during the scholastic era. By the time of Thomas Aquinas, the theology of the cosmic Christ had developed through building upon the central notion of *theosis* or divinisation, that was first expressed in the Eastern Fathers. The stress in cosmic Christology was not only upon the notion of Christ as present in the whole of the cosmos, but also that through Christ's incarnation the whole of the cosmos is able to share in the divine nature of God.

> Each creature is a witness to God's power and omnipotence; and its beauty is a witness to the divine wisdom.... Every creature participates in some way in the likeness of the Divine Essence.... The Incarnation accomplished the following: That God became human and that humans became God and sharers in the divine nature (Aquinas quoted in Fox 1988:75).

Of course the development of cosmic Christology continued in various stages throughout Christian history, too many to cover within the scope of this book, in fact the development of this theology still continues today. As has already been discussed in some detail, a recent, and significant, contributor to this doctrine is Pierre Teilhard de Chardin. Teilhard's view, like Origen's, brings weaves an understanding of Christ with the evolutionary nature of the cosmos, in a manner that shows the cosmic Christ not only as the source and sustainer of all that exists, but also the ultimate goal of all creation. What makes Teilhard's approach to this doctrine all the more notable is his suggestion that the cosmic aspect of Christology is far more significant than had previously been acknowledged in the Christian faith. This point has not been considered in significant critical detail in contemporary scholarship, but Teilhard, suggests that Christ actually has a third nature, that is, a cosmic nature. Teilhard writes: "This third nature of Christ (neither human nor divine, but cosmic) – has not noticeably attracted the explicit attention of the faithful or of theologians" (Teilhard quoted in Fox 1988:77). Lyons extrapolates Teilhard's contribution to the doctrine of the cosmic Christ.

> As the one who holds all things together, Christ exercises a supremacy over the universe which is physical, not simply juridical. He is the unifying centre of the universe and its goal. The function of holding all things together indicates that Christ is not only man and God; he also possesses a third aspect - indeed, a third nature - which is cosmic (Lyons 1982:153).

From the preceding discussion on the development of this doctrine one is able to extract three seminal emphases that have arisen - although these are not necessarily to be considered chronological, or linear, emphases. First, from biblical and natural revelation comes the understanding of Christ as the source and sustainer of the whole cosmos. Second, there is the bridging of the radical distinction between creator and creation, leading to the notion that Christ is present in all creation – and by his presence he sanctifies and divinises the whole cosmos. The third aspect is the understanding that the whole of the cosmos has Christ as its ultimate goal.

Naturally Fr Bede was aware of these emphases in Teilhard's theology, and so what is of importance for this book is the way in which Fr Bede uses and understands the term cosmic Christ, as well as the way in which he emphasises and develops it. Even though the section above shows that the doctrine of the cosmic Christ developed throughout Christian history, it has sadly been neglected in recent centuries. This is largely as a result of the impact of Newtonian science and its influence upon the world-view of the hitherto dominant West in scholarship. Thus Fr Bede's emphasis on this aspect of Christology serves as a necessary corrective within the Christian faith. Moreover, what makes his cosmic Christology so insightful and valuable is his emphasis on the primacy of experience. However, this also presents some challenges to his readers since the communication of experience is never able to fully convey the depth and complexity of the experience itself. It is because of this challenge that this book has suggested that Fr Bede is constantly moving between two 'horizons'. The one horizon is that of his experience of the cosmic Christ – an element that arises from the mystical influence of Hinduism on his faith. This experience is beyond a conclusive, entirely accurate, doctrinal and philosophical expression since it is primarily mystical in nature. The other horizon is that of Fr Bede's expression and articulation of his experience using words and concepts that can only convey the mystery of this reality in part.

One of the primary struggles in Fr Bede's cosmic Christology is his desire to communicate both the unity and distinction that exist between creation and creator. Language is unable to express fully the experience of true unity in distinction without weakening the emphasis on unity when stressing distinction, and vice versa. For the Christian, creation, including human persons, and so also to some extent the incarnate Christ, is not merely a manifestation of God (as in the case of an *avatara* in Hinduism). Rather, creation differs in its very nature from God who created it. Creation differs in its very nature from God in that its nature is that of the creation of a creator God. Yet, at the same time while there is distinction between creator and creation the two are not ontologically separate from each other – since how can anything possibly exist outside of the God who is? Thus, there is a clear distinction, but not a radical separation.

This problem leads Fr Bede to use the term 'cosmic' in two senses. The first way in which Fr Bede uses the term cosmic (in reference to his cosmic Christology) has strong ties and links to the Christian faith and its doctrines, while this second usage of the term has a range that stretches beyond conventional Christianity.

First, he uses the term cosmic in the sense of the created order or cosmos. Of this creation he writes:

> But for the Christian there is a creation, which is not simply a "manifestation" of God, but a real creation in the sense which has been explained, which differs in its very nature from God, that is, which has a created being which is essentially different from the being of God (Griffiths 1973:53).

Thus, on one level when Fr Bede speaks of the cosmos in relation to Christ he is referring to all that has been created by the creator and is distinct in nature from that creator. The dilemma that arises from this distinction is that if taken to the extreme it could suggest a radical separation between creator and creation. However, Fr Bede uses his cosmic Christology to overcome this difficulty. He does this by emphasising that while God is distinct from creation, God, in Christ, is also within creation. Reflecting on his own experience of this reality Fr Bede writes that, "God is to be seen in the earth and in the whole creation" (1992:96). Thus, when he refers to the cosmic Christ in this sense, he is referring to the continuing creative and sustaining activity of Christ as present in creation. "In him and through him and for him all things are created and in him all things hold together" (Colossians 1:16). In short, this usage of the term has primarily to do with the relationship between Christ and material reality.

Fr Bede employs the term cosmic Christ in a second manner. Here he speaks of the cosmic Christ who is "beyond space and time, is totally one with the Father, the creator God, and so is also present in creation" (1992:96). This is the transcendent element of his cosmic

Christology. Here Fr Bede moves from using the notion of the cosmic Christ in relation only to material or physical reality to further include the psychological and spiritual aspects of reality. In relating and expressing this aspect of his experience of the cosmic Christ, Fr Bede draws on a wide range of disciplines, cultures and religions. It is because of this second understanding of the cosmic Christ that Fr Bede has been able to encounter, and be encountered by, people of others faiths and cultures. He maintained with passion that the cosmic Christ, in this broader usage of the term, is "present in all religion", and that "Jesus died for all humanity without exception" (1992:96).

Taking his usage of the cosmic Christ further, in this second sense, Fr Bede sees Christ not only as having significance for all physical reality, but truly having significance for all reality, physical, psychological and spiritual (cf. Griffiths 1992:96-97). The key to the cosmic Christ's significance for all reality is to be found in Fr Bede's emphasis upon the transformation of the cosmos. In line with other cosmic Christologies Fr Bede emphasises that Christ, through his incarnation, life and ascension, is constantly bringing the divine life of God into creation, and drawing the cosmos into the divine life of God. The cosmic Christ is that Person who holds all creation together and creates it moment by moment. This transformation, in Christian terms, as it is found in Fr Bede's spirituality, is influenced by Teilhard de Chardin's evolutionary view of the cosmos as moving towards 'Christ consciousness' – the goal of all creation (cf. Griffiths 1989:92-95).

In concluding this section on the way in which Fr Bede approaches and utilises the notion of the cosmic Christ, it must be noted that neither of these two uses, the Christian nor the mystical / spiritual usage, expressed above, are entirely novel. As mentioned in the introduction to this section, the understanding of Christ as creator, sustainer and goal of the whole cosmos (spiritual, physical and psychological) has become a common understanding within cosmic Christology. However, there are two things that make Fr Bede's cosmic Christology particularly valuable and significant. The first is the primacy of experience, in this case experiencing the cosmic Christ. Well-formulated doctrine must always be understood as an expression of a far greater reality, a reality that can only be experienced beyond the confines of language and human reason – after all, a cornerstone of theology is not that we discover truth about God, but rather that God reveals such truth to us. This leads to the second valuable contribution

that Fr Bede makes to continuing development of cosmic Christology:
Fr Bede shifts the boundaries of contemporary Christian doctrine, as
will be shown below, by moving beyond the confines of the traditional
language and philosophy associated with Christology and drawing on a
wide range of disciplines, religions and cultures, to communicate and
express his experience of the cosmic Christ.

The next section of this chapter will examine the way in which Fr
Bede has enriched his cosmic Christology by relating it to, and
expressing it through, Indian (and particularly Hindu), cultural and
religious expressions in greater detail.

Christ in India

As the passage in the introduction of this chapter illustrates, the
concept of incarnate deity is nothing new to India. In fact
contemporary Hindus suggest that every age has an incarnation.
According to Fr Bede the most renowned (in the sense of being most
famous) incarnation during his lifetime was Satya Sai Baba (1987:67).
At a later stage in this chapter there will be a discussion on some
significant differences between the Hindu and Christian concepts of
incarnation. Here however, one need only note that incarnation, in a
broad sense, is not unknown to the Indian religious mindset.

It is interesting to note a theological shift that took place within Fr
Bede's theology over his life. Initially, it was Fr Bede's intention to go
to India in order to establish a Benedictine monastery, and in so doing
take Christ to India. However, upon his arrival in India he discovered
that Christ was already there in a very real sense, not only through the
Church, but also present in the lives of very many devout people. So,
instead of going to India merely to impart and share his faith, Fr Bede
came to a new discovery of God, the Church and Christ by allowing
the rich presence of Christ in India, its people and religion, to
influence, shape, and inform him (1982:7). Valiaveetil suggests that Fr
Bede builds his Indian Christology on the basis of "the deepest
experience of the Absolute in the Hindu and Christian
traditions" (1997:9). Accordingly, Fr Bede is able to draw on the
strengths and insights of both Hindu and Christian spirituality and
doctrine in expressing his experience of the Absolute. Valiaveetil notes
how valuable the complementarity of such an approach is when
writing:

> The Hindu experience springs from the contemplation of
> the cosmos, from the human experience of the physical
> and the psychic world.... The Christian experience of
> the Absolute has its basis in the Person of Jesus Christ
> (1997:9)

Commenting on the worth of his experience in the East, and how it has
enriched his spirituality and theology, Fr Bede said that when

> ... the Christian faith is seen from the Oriental
> perspective, another aspect of Truth contained in the
> original revelation is disclosed (1982:26).

Arising from his developing discovery Fr Bede interpreted and
expressed the doctrine of Christ in the light of eastern linguistic and
theological concepts; in this process he came to realise more fully the
extent to which Christ was truly present in India (cf. Griffiths
1984:218-223 for an early account of Fr Bede's awakening to the
presence of the "Unknown Christ of Hinduism").

The East has a different understanding of God, and would
therefore be expected to have a different understanding of the second
person of the Trinity, Jesus Christ. In India Fr Bede discovered an
ethos of God-consciousness that permeates all life. In essence this
understanding maintains that all of the cosmos is sacred, an emphasis
that became an essential element in the formulation of his cosmic
Christology (1982:15-16). In a broad sense knowledge of God in the
East is far more intuitive, and much less rational, than is the norm in
western theology. This is in part because knowledge of God, in the
East, is much more a matter of experiencing God than a matter of
doctrinal formulation about God. As a sannyasi in India Fr Bede's
cosmic Christology was fundamentally influenced by this mystical
approach, particularly as he came to discover and incorporate his
experiences into his theology.

What follows is a focus on the most significant Hindu influences
on Fr Bede's cosmic Christology. Foremost among these is the notion
of the cosmic Person.

The cosmic Person - *purusha*

To some extent Fr Bede's relationship with other religions was
influenced, as a Catholic, by the stance of the Second Vatican Council

which held that the "Church rejects nothing that is true and holy in other religions" (in Griffiths 1992:96). Thus in accordance with the widely-accepted position of the Second Vatican Council Fr Bede had a positive view of other non-Christian religions[18]. The opening passage of *Lumen Gentium* states:

> In Christ the Church is a kind of sacrament, that is to say it is a sign and instrument of the intimate union with God and the unity of all mankind (in Gaybba 1981:87).

This notion of the Church as a sacrament that has universal significance for all people and faiths is not that far removed from Fr Bede's understanding of the person and work of Christ as "mythical symbol" with efficacy for all people and all of creation (Griffiths 1983:129-130 see also chapter three). However, as will be shown, Fr Bede went far beyond the official stance of the Second Vatican Council on other religions. It is certainly clear from Fr Bede's later works that he viewed Christ as significant for all religions. In his early works he maintains that all religion contains truth leading up to Christ, in much the same way that Clement of Alexandria saw Greek philosophy as a *praeparatio evangelica* (a preparation for the coming of the Gospel). Fr Bede writes:

> Thus there is a solid tradition according to which Christianity, that is to say the mystery of Christ and the Church, can be said to have existed from the beginning of the world. It is present in creation, because the whole creation finds its meaning and its purpose in Christ, who assumes the whole material universe in the life of God. It is present in all history, because Christ comes as the 'fulfilment' of history and reveals the nature of human destiny. Above all, it is found in the different religious traditions of the world, because in them this 'mystery' is gradually unfolded... [in these religions] we have so many 'prophecies' as it were of the mystery of Christ. (Griffiths 1984:220).

Here again one is able to detect the significant influence that Teilhard de Chardin's cosmic Christology had on Fr Bede's theological and spiritual development. Teilhard maintained that Christ is the 'omega', or goal, of creation, and as such, the goal of all religion (cf. Teilhard de Chardin 1965:54-56). Lyons offers a synopsis of Teilhard's view, saying that according to Teilhard, "the world has only one goal of creation, Omega, the supernatural goal, which is Christ" (Lyons 1982:158). As stated earlier (chapter three) Teilhard's view is evolutionary in content. Lyons suggests that for Teilhard the transformation of the Cosmos (cosmogenesis) can only be fully expressed in "Christic transformation" (expressed as Christogenesis) (1982:155). Valiaveetil observes that Fr Bede's view of the evolution of consciousness finds resonance with both Teilhard's notion of the 'omega point' and with what Sri Aurobindo[19] calls the 'gnostic being' or 'superman' (1997:9). In his writings Fr Bede adopted aspects of both Aurobindo and Teilhard's evolutionary models for the transformation of creation particularly in relation to the evolution of consciousness (see the explanation of Teilhard's 'forces analogy' in chapter three).

> So as the universe continues to evolve, the relative importance of the tangential force decreases while the importance of the radial force increases. The radial force for Teilhard is spirit and he speaks of it as Christ-consciousness. As the universe matures the intensity of this radial force of Christ-consciousness increases exponentially, being continuously contributed to and reinforced by all the centuries of consciousness in the universe (Griffiths 1989:26).

Thus, for Fr Bede, as for Teilhard de Chardin, the cosmic Christ is both the source and goal of all creation. However, with regard to the significance of the cosmic Christ for religion, Fr Bede often made use of an illustration (quoted below) to explain his view.

> The Christian mission is to help other people grow but also to learn from them so that our Christian faith grows too.... Our aim is the deepening of our own faith which then becomes more open to others. This is not easy, and everybody has to answer the question themselves. I like the illustration of fingers and the palm of the hand. The fingers represent Buddhism, Hinduism, Islam, Judaism and Christianity. Buddhism is miles from Christianity, and each has its own position. If you try and mix them, taking a bit of Hinduism or Buddhism and adding Christianity, that is syncretism. But if you

go deeply into any one tradition you converge on
the centre, and there you see how we all come forth
from a common root (Griffiths 1992:96-97[20]).

From the above it is clear to see that Fr Bede's understanding of
religious development fits into the broad 'perennialist' understanding
of all religion as originating from a common source. For Fr Bede
Christ is this source; he notes that, "Christ is ultimately the source of
all religion. He is behind it all" (1992:97). Such an understanding is
complex in that it needs to incorporate an understanding of Christ as
the true source of all religion that predates the Christian faith. It is in
this regard that Fr Bede's understanding of cosmic or universal
revelation is so important (see the explanation of this in chapter three if
you have not already done so).

Fr Bede agrees with the understanding that the mystery of Christ
has existed since before the foundation of the world (see quotation
above from Griffiths 1984:220). The theological starting point of this
notion is to be found in the teaching of the Apostle Paul. According to
Paul the whole creation takes place "in Christ", "For by him all things
were created: things in heaven and on earth, visible and invisible,
whether thrones or powers or rulers or authorities; all things were
created by him and for him. He is before all things, and in him all
things hold together" (Colossians1:16-17). This means that we cannot
properly think of anything apart from Christ, as Fr Bede insists
(1992:97). It is Christ who gives existence and meaning to all that
exists. Here Fr Bede is speaking of the pre-incarnate Christ, the *logos*
spoken of in John 1:1-2 and a number of other New Testament texts.

Thus far the discussion of Fr Bede's understanding of the
cosmic Person has focussed only on the insights that can be gained
from Christian theology[21]. An essential element to understanding Fr
Bede's cosmic Christology is a discussion of the way in which he
relates the above-mentioned aspects of Christian doctrine to the
Hindu doctrine of the *purusha*. The word *purusha* can be translated
as 'man', 'cosmic man', 'cosmic person' or 'archetypal person' (cf.
Griffiths 1989:128).

The idea of an archetypal or cosmic Person is developed most
clearly in Hinduism, although it can also be found in Buddhism and
Islam. The Rig Veda states, "this purusha is all that has been and all
that will be, the Lord of immortality" (in Griffiths 1989:128).

Furthermore, the Rig Veda says that the *purusha* is both immanent in, and transcends all, creation. "One fourth of Him is here on earth, three-fourths are above in heaven" (quoted in Griffiths 1983:74). Fr Bede suggests that the one fourth of the *purusha* that is immanent on earth manifests everything that is, including human persons. The three fourths are the dimension of "his being above in heaven" (1983:75). As such the *purusha* is both the person from whom all creation comes and the one who sustains, and forms, all creation.

Fr Bede suggests that it is very probable that Jesus identified himself with the primordial or cosmic Person in saying "... before Abraham was I am" (John 8:58).

> The primordial man was before Abraham and before all men, and I think it is very probable that Jesus is identifying himself there with this primordial or heavenly man, who is prior to all creation. (Griffiths 1989:120).

Fr Bede takes this notion further, as do many New Testament scholars, in saying that Jesus identifies himself with the Son of Man figure from the Book of Enoch. This book was written a short time before Jesus and was almost certainly in circulation during Christ's earthly life. Accordingly, Fr Bede notes that it is highly likely that its contents would have been familiar to Christ. In the Book of Enoch the Son of Man appears and is identified with the "Ancient of Days" who is the primordial or cosmic Person who existed before creation (cf. Griffiths 1989:120). The Book of Enoch also says that the Son of Man was hidden from the world and would be manifest at the end of time. This links him with the Son of Man image that is to be found in the book of Daniel.

In Daniel, the Son of Man is said to have existed from the beginning but would come at the *eschaton* or fullness of time. The Son of Man in Enoch is also viewed as the promised Messiah who was to come. Fr Bede feels that this further corroborates the idea that Jesus would have viewed himself in these terms as the primordial person, the Son of Man and the transcendent Messiah who was to come (Griffiths 1989:121). This is in line with the fact that in the Gospels Jesus never speaks of himself as God. In fact, His most common designation of himself is Son of Man.

Another remarkable insight that comes from the notion of *purusha* is that of the sacrifice of the cosmic Person. At the beginning of time the *purusha* is sacrificed and his limbs are scattered over the world. In ritual sacrifice *purusha* is gathered together and becomes one again. According to Fr Bede this has a profound correlation in the concept of Adam and the Son of Man. St Augustine said that "Adam, at the fall, was scattered over all the earth" (quoted in Griffiths 1983:75). Fr Bede's commentary on this is that humanity

> ... was once one, one with nature, one with himself, one with God. And then when he fell he was scattered and divided. The atonement means that God comes into this divided universe and gathers those scattered pieces together and in his sacrifice reunites mankind. He brings all persons together in his Person (1983:75).

Just as the *purusha,* the cosmic Person of the Vedas, once sacrificed is made whole again, so too one can see this taking place in the Christian concept of the atonement. God enters the universe and gathers divided and scattered persons and makes them one in his Person. Augustine writes, "In the end there will *unus Christus amans seipsum* - One Christ loving himself in all his members" (quoted in Griffiths 1983:75). Jesus is the lamb that was slain before the creation of the world, as with the Hindu concept of the *purusha*. Fr Bede says that it is in this regard that Jesus sees himself as the Son of Man. As suggested in the book of Daniel, the Son of Man is the one that comes at the end of time to fulfil God's plan for the unity of creation (1989:118). The cosmic Person who comes in the fullness of time to be a sacrifice, is the one that makes all reality, the entire cosmos, whole again.

Fr Bede's cosmic Christology further draws on the widely accepted view that Jesus identified himself with the 'suffering servant' of Isaiah 53 (1989:119). Jesus is not only the Son of Man that comes on the clouds of heaven (Matthew 26:63-64), but also the suffering servant that gives life to the world. Jesus speaks of himself as a representative of all people (Matthew 25:40), just as the suffering servant of Isaiah is representative of Israel. Jesus is the *purusha*, the cosmic Person, the one who is before all creation, yet who comes at the end as the Son of Man to redeem all creation. He is the suffering servant who gathers all things up under One head (Ephesians 1:10), taking all that is scattered and divided and making it One.

This section has shown how Fr Bede's understanding of the doctrine and work of Christ is enriched by the Hindu doctrine of the *purusha*. His theological formulation goes a long way towards expressing the doctrine of Christ in a manner that would be far more acceptable to the eastern mindset. He comments:

> In India there is today an attempt to create an Indian Christian Theology. We seek to express our Christian faith in the language of Vedanta as the Greek Fathers expressed it in the language of Plato and Aristotle. Purusha will be one of the key words in an Indian Christian Theology (1983:76).

His contribution to an innovative Christology cannot be discounted. Fr Bede's approach and sensitivity to the culture and religions of the East can serve as an example to theologians and Christians in many parts of the world who are attempting to form a faith that is inculturated. The significance of these steps will be discussed in some detail in the next chapter of this book. Next, however, this chapter will discuss the relationship between the cosmic Christ and the created order.

Christ and creation

For Christians the doctrine of the incarnation is central to understanding Christ's person and work. The second article of the Nicea-Constantinople Creed (381 AD) expresses this clearly as it gives a synopsis of the Christian doctrine of the person and work of Christ. It says (in paraphrase) that Jesus is the only Son of God, begotten from the Father. Moreover, Jesus is true God from true God, creator of all things. It also affirms that Jesus became a human person for the salvation of creation, being born of the Virgin Mary.

This section will discuss how Fr Bede interprets the incarnation of Christ in his cosmic Christology, and highlight new insights of this aspect of Christian doctrine, as well as the significance of it for our faith. For the sake of clarity it will be necessary to order this discussion under a number of separate headings.

Jesus: Self-knowledge of the Father

The archetypal man is said to have been created (or in the case of Christianity, begotten) in the image of God. Fr Bede deals with this understanding of Christ as the image of the Father (or God) in his explanation of the Trinity as *saccidananda* (1982:190).

In explaining *saccidananda* Fr Bede says that the Father is *sat*, meaning True Being, the source of all that exists. Everything that exists does so in the Being of the Father who is the source of all exists. The Son is *chit*, meaning knowledge. As such the Son is the knowledge of the Father and exists within the Being (or mind) of God. The Holy Spirit is *ananda*, the bliss of love between Father and Son and Son and Father, uniting each to the other and to creation. Returning to the notion of the Son as *chit*, Fr Bede further understood that the Son as knowledge of the Father is, "... Being reflecting on itself, knowing itself, expressing itself in the eternal Word" (Griffiths 1982:190). All creation comes into being through the manifestation of the Father in the Son. Within Fr Bede's Indian Christian theology the Son would be

> ... *Saguna Brahman*, Brahman 'with attributes', as Creator, Lord, Saviour, the Self-manifestation of the unmanifest God, the personal aspect of the Godhead, the *Purusha* (1982:190).

Within traditional Christology the Son is said to be the image of the invisible God, or the *eikon tou theou*, to use the words of the New Testament (cf. 2 Corinthians 4:4). Jesus is not the Father. He always remains the Son, even though he is of one substance with the Father. Christian doctrine would suggest that Jesus is the *morphē tou theou*, the manifestation, the form or the nature of God as spoken of by Paul in Philippians 2:6. Fr Bede points out that the word *morphē*, form, is from the same root as the Sanskrit word *murti* (Griffiths 1989:122). This means Jesus is the image or form of God, the Self-Knowledge of the Father through whom all creation comes into being. When the Source of all reflects on Self, it expresses Self in the form of an eternal Self-Knowing and Self-Revealing word, the *logos* of John's Gospel (cf. John 1:1-3). Thus Jesus the *logos* of God can be likened to the *purusha* of the Bhagavad Gita, as the Self-knowledge of the source with attributes (*saguna brahman*), that is to say the Son with attributes, is a reflection upon the source who transcends all reasonable human description and characterisation (*nirguna brahman*) (cf. Griffiths 1982:190). Fr Bede suggests that Colossians 1:15-17 points this out quite clearly.

> He is the image of the invisible God, the firstborn over
> all creation. For by him all things were created: things in
> heaven and on earth, visible and invisible, whether
> thrones or powers or rulers or authorities, all things were
> created by him and for him. He is before all things and
> in him all things hold together. (NIV).

He suggests that this understanding of Jesus as the cosmic Person or
cosmic Lord, "who is God's self-manifestation to the world, gives us
the key to the New Testament understanding of the relation of Jesus to
God" (1989:124) and as such enriches our understanding of both the
person of Christ and the doctrine of the Trinity.

Valiaveetil observes of this aspect of Fr Bede's cosmic Christology
that, "In Christ's consciousness of unity with the Father we have the
basis of Christian Advaita. It is a non-dual experience, but an
experience of unity in distinction, of oneness with
difference" (1997:8). Here again one can see where Teilhard de
Chardin's theology has influenced Fr Bede's. Fr Bede sums up his
view of Christ's unity in distinction with the Father in the following
manner:

> ...here [referring to John 17:21] Jesus reveals this inner
> mystery of his oneness with the Father. This to me is the
> climax of it all, that this Son of Man, this man knows
> Himself in this unity with the Father. He can say, "I and
> the Father are one." And that is the mystery of unity in
> distinction. This is the point that is generally missed.
> Jesus does not say, "I am the Father." That would be
> pure advaita, pure identity, but he says rather, "I and the
> Father are one," which is unity in distinction... And he
> also says, "I am in the Father, and the Father is in me."
> That is the proper way of expressing the advaita in
> Christian terms (Griffiths quoted in Valiaveetil 1997:8).

Thus, it can be safely said that for Fr Bede the Trinity as understood
within the framework of Christian advaita reveals the mystery of unity
in distinction. Jesus' very identity is advaitic, and this non-dual
relationship is cosmic in that it extends to all creation. Fr Bede
expressed this notion in saying that

> ...the Word is the self-expression, the self-knowledge of
> God, and the Spirit is the self-communication of His
> being. And just as God knows Himself in the whole

> creation he has made, so He loves Himself (in it). The
> Spirit is present in the whole creation... In a real sense,
> we are loved into existence by God (Griffiths in
> Valiaveetil 1997:8).

Therefore, to sum up, in his identity as self-knowledge of the Father,
the cosmic Christ reveals the true nature of unity in distinction. In this
relationship we see truly the reconciliation of the One and many, the
cosmic significance of the Son's filial unity with the Father.

Jesus: Fully God, fully human

The Council of Nicea, in 325 AD, affirmed the doctrine that Jesus is
fully God and fully human in one person, one *ousia* (person) in two
hypostaseis (natures). While Fr Bede (1989:113) agrees with the
outcome of the council, he emphasises the proposition of many biblical
scholars, who maintain that Jesus is not presented as fully God in the
New Testament.

Fr Bede holds that the New Testament does not start from the
premise of Jesus as God, but from the premise of Jesus as human (i.e.,
Jesus the man of Nazareth). He also shows that Jesus never speaks of
himself as God, rather he refers to himself as the Son of Man, which in
Hebrew and Aramaic is practically equivalent to man (or human) as
has been suggested above (1989:113). He goes further in saying that it
is only after his death that his disciples begin to ask the question who
this Man was and interpret his life and message in the light of the
Jewish tradition. Thus, Fr Bede notes that it is only at the end of the
New Testament period that the disciples begin to refer to Jesus as God;
and that the assertion that Jesus is Lord is based, on reflection, upon
Christ's person and message and particularly upon his resurrection (cf.
Griffiths 1989:113-114). Moreover, Fr Bede cautions that an
unqualified use of the word 'God' in relation to Jesus can be
dangerous. He feels that it could cause a great deal of confusion,
particularly if seen from the perspective of other religious traditions
(1989:114). For the Muslim to say that a man, Jesus, is God, would be
the 'ultimate blasphemy'. Such an assertion would associate a creature
with the creator and thus deny the absolute transcendence of the one
God. This is the one extreme. For the Hindu there is also danger, in
that the Hindu may take the notion of Jesus as God to the other
extreme. Fr Bede sums up the difficulty with this concept in relation to
Hinduism in saying that for a Hindu "there is no difficulty in speaking

of Jesus as God since in Hinduism every human being is potentially divine and anyone who has realised his divinity is entitled to be called God or *Bhagavan*" (1989:114).

Thus, the Hindu may have no problem with seeing Jesus as an *avatara*, an incarnation of God. However, here a major problem arises for the Christian when the incarnation of Christ is related to the Hindu notion of incarnation. Unlike an *avatara*, Jesus is not merely one of many forms in which God has appeared on earth. As will be discussed later, Jesus is *the* incarnation of God, not merely an incarnation of God, among many other incarnations of God.

However, to return to the discussion of Jesus as fully God and fully human, Fr Bede held that in the New Testament Jesus is not precisely God in an unqualified sense. He is, as mentioned in the section above, the Word of God, the Image of God, the Self-revelation and manifestation of God, "who is reflected in the whole creation and brings the whole creation back to God" (1989:126-127). The nearest that the New Testament comes to saying that Jesus is God, is to be found in the prologue of John's Gospel. Here it says that the Word (*logos*) who became flesh both was God (*theos*) and was in relation to God (*pros ton theon*) (Griffiths 1989:127). It is important not to misunderstand what Fr Bede is saying about Jesus being God. What he says is that it is

> ... therefore perfectly correct to say that Jesus is God, but always with the qualification that he is 'God from God', that is, he receives the Godhead from the Father, which is what characterises him as the Son; and furthermore he is not simply God, but God in man and man in God. (Griffiths 1989:127).

Fr Bede's understanding of the cosmic Christ as the Self-revelation of the Father thus emphasises both the nature of Christ as God of God, and his full humanity as a person. In many respects this aspect of Fr Bede's Christology shows how he maintains traditional thoughts on the person of Christ. Hence, the cosmic Christ that Fr Bede experienced and the Christ of whom Fr Bede speaks is not foreign to Christianity and its doctrine, although in some other places, his expression of the doctrine of Christ does transcend the boundaries of traditional Christian doctrine, through his use of Hindu theological concepts and language.

Jesus in history and his full humanity

The next essential element in Fr Bede's cosmic Christology is the relationship between Christ and history and how this shows that Christ is fully human. As argued above, Jesus is God of God who enters into creation, once, in the concrete historical context of human history. This derives from the fact that the Christian tradition comes out of the Hebrew faith with its concept of time. The Hebrew tradition has an understanding of time as linear. There are certain historical events that are of fundamental importance to the Hebrew faith (Griffiths 1983:175). An example is the historical importance of the Exodus from Egypt, going through the desert and into the promised land. According to this linear view of time, all time moves according to a divine plan, and is moving towards an end point (*eschaton*). It is held that God reveals God's self not only in nature, but also in history, in relationships with particular historical groups and people and in the events that take place in their lives (cf. Wong 1996:2).

In this sense Christianity derives from the historical event of Jesus Christ who was born in a particular time and place, lived and died.

> This is what is specific in the Christian mystical experience. The absolute reality is experienced as revealed in Christ, in the life and death of Jesus of Nazareth. It is not an experience of absolute reality revealed in the Cosmos, in the cycle of time in nature, nor in the human Self, the psychic being with its capacity for self-transcendence, but in a historic person and a historic event (Griffiths 1983:179).

The true significance of this is that God is fully incarnate in a historical person, Jesus Christ. God enters fully into our human experience. The bible points out that Jesus knew pain and suffering, as well as joy. He knew the limitations and restrictions, as well as the weaknesses, of human nature. These human attributes and experiences are an important distinction between notions of incarnation in Christianity and Hinduism (cf. chapter four). Christ enters into creation fully as a human person. He was "one who has been tempted in every way, just as we are--yet was without sin" (Hebrews 4:15). Jesus overcame the sin and weakness of humanity both as the historical and as the cosmic Person. He brings all things together in himself (Ephesians 1:10), and in the resurrection takes all of creation into the Godhead once and for all. Fr Bede maintained, as most Christians do, that this was a once-off event that cannot be repeated (Wong 1996:3).

This is a key distinction between Christianity and Hinduism. Fr Bede employs the notion of 'symbol' to describe the historical significance of the Christ event.

> The death and resurrection of Christ is a unique event. In one sense it is a mythological event, an event of supreme symbolism. It is a sign of God's salvation for the whole creation and the whole of humanity (Griffiths 1983:125).

Essential to understanding how the historical work of Christ functions as a symbol of salvation is an understanding of the difference between historical and cosmic revelation (see chapter three for a discussion on this). Fr Bede sums up the difference as follows.

> The fundamental difference between the Hebrew and the Hindu Revelation is that the latter is the revelation of God's work in creation, and the former is the revelation of God's work in history, the history of a particular people (1983:120).

Rama and Krishna are thus mythical symbols that have a universal meaning for all creation, and they belong to cyclic time. By contrast, Jesus is a symbol who reveals God as rooted in history and creation. He is a human person, a part of the created order (even though he was not created). Fr Bede says that the life, death and resurrection of Jesus are events of supreme symbolism in that they serve as a sign of God's salvation for all of creation and the whole of humanity (1983:125). However, the life, death and resurrection of Jesus are not only important as a sign of salvation, they are also concrete acts that change history. These aspects are important as an historical event in that not only do the life, death and resurrection of Jesus Christ have a message of salvation for the whole cosmos, they also have a concrete effect on history.

> The divine life penetrates history, time, suffering, and death, and then raises history and time and suffering and death into a new creation, a new order of being in which these things are not lost, not destroyed, but transfigured (Griffiths 1983:127).

God becoming fully human, in the person of Jesus, is a symbol of the new creation. As God enters history in human form he divinises creation, sanctifying it by His human presence. As the fully human Jesus ascends into the Godhead he completes this act by reuniting creation to its source and taking matter into God. This is only possible through God becoming fully human and entering into history.

Buddha, Krishna and Christ

The earlier section entitled, 'Christ in India', pointed out that incarnation is not a foreign concept to India. Hindus would say that every age has an incarnation or *avatara*. In fact many gurus in India proclaim themselves to be avatars. Fr Bede cites Satya Sai Baba as a contemporary example of just such a person, who claims to be the supreme *avatara* beyond Jesus, Buddha and Krishna (Griffiths 1987:67). In classical tradition however, there are only ten avatars, the final (tenth) one being Kalki who comes at the end of the world to bring all things to a conclusion (Griffiths 1983:124). It is worth noting that Christ would be regarded as an *avatara* by most modern Hindus. Some may then ask, could not speak of him as the final *avatara* among others? Fr Bede would say no.

The Hindu doctrine of the *avatara* and the Christian concept of incarnation are in fact very different in many ways. Fr Bede says, first that an *avatara* is based on a myth rather than history (1987:67). The fish, the boar and tortoise are all mythological figures. Even Rama and Krishna are only semi-historical. Fr Bede says there may have been historical persons, Rama and Krishna, but as avatars they are more like Hector or Achilles, the heroes of Greek epics. They may have existed as people, but the stories that have grown up around them are legendary rather than historical (1987:67).

A further difference between Christ and Krishna has to do with the strong moral emphasis associated with God, and all that is associated with God, in the Judeo-Christian traditions. Valiaveetil notes that Krishna is known for the quality of ecstatic love and for "somewhat questionable behaviour toward the Gopis which seems to show him in an immoral light" (1997:9). However, in the historical person of Christ there is no such moral ambiguity. Jesus Christ represents the epitome of moral perfection and holiness, which is widely viewed by Christians as a primary characteristic of God himself. Fr Bede says:

> The love of God was revealed in Christ not in poetry, but
> in history. It was shown not in ecstasy, but in self-giving
> for others, in the surrender of his life on the cross
> (1976:83).

The third, and most significant difference between incarnation and *avatara* is that the concept of *avatara* is a theophany rather than in incarnation (as understood in Christian terms). A theophany fits comfortably into a cyclic notion of time. In Indian philosophy time is conceived as moving in cycles. The world comes from *brahman*, goes through all the cycles of life and in the end it returns to *brahman*. Then the cycle starts again. In this view of time there is no real beginning and end, no finality. Each time righteousness declines the *avatara* appears temporarily and then disappears when his task is complete. Thus the *avatara* appears again and again on earth in some form or another, throughout the cycles of time (Griffiths 1983:124-125).

For the Christian, the whole point of the incarnation is that Jesus came at the end of the age to bring all things to completion (Ephesians 1:10). There is finality in this event. It is an event that takes place in history and announces the beginning of God's ultimate end. Christ is God incarnate, not merely a theophany. In contrast to the cyclic view of time, the Judeo-Christian view is linear. All things progress towards an end, the *eschaton* where history is fulfilled. The incarnation is part of this plan and takes place in history.

The avatara is conceived as a *lila* (play) of God. The Christian could never speak of the terrible suffering of the crucifixion of Christ as *lila*[22] (Griffiths 1987:69). However, it must be noted that lila, as understood in the context of the Gita, does refer to the purposeful activity of God. Such a view would be more consistent with the Christian understanding of the redemptive work of Christ (cf. Griffiths 1987:69, 87). Nonetheless, the Hindu and Christian emphasis on history and the Hindu understanding of it, in relation to the activity of God, highlight an important difference. For Christians, history has a definite meaning and purpose, not only in the events themselves, but also in the sequence and chronology of the events. The purpose, meaning and plan of history are fully revealed in the human Person of Jesus Christ and the events of his life, death and resurrection. Jesus is indeed God become fully human, unlike Krishna, Buddha and other avatars who are theophanies. The difference here is that Jesus is fully human – with all that that means soteriologically, and the Hindu avatars are not. Jesus is God who brings fulfilment to God's plan for humanity and creation (Griffiths 1987:69).

Conclusion

Fr Bede's cosmic Christology is a central aspect in his spirituality. It is the axis around which he discusses the relationship between creator and creation. It also forms the foundation of his desire for interfaith encounter leading to the goal of mutual enrichment by transcending boundaries and hindrances between the faiths. Creating such common ground between the faiths is clearly in line with his understanding of Christian advaita. Wong comments on the importance of Fr Bede's cosmic Christology in the following manner.

> The special goal of the Incarnation, according to Bede, is to lead humans into a new state of consciousness and relationship with God, that is, to participate in Jesus' filial consciousness and his intimacy with the Father. This is the source of a Christian advaita.... The distinctive nature of the Christian revelation, its historical and world-affirming character, has been constantly upheld by Bede, while the advaitic mystical experience of the Trinity, or Saccidananda, has been presented as the profound common ground for dialogue with Hinduism. These various aspects can be found in the person of Jesus Christ (1996:6).

There is a great deal that one can learn from this innovative approach to the doctrine of Christ. I believe that this understanding of the doctrine of the cosmic Christ emphasises, in a profound way, *inter alia*, the manner in which Christ not only creates, but also permeates all creation with his divine presence. He is truly the one who creates, and holds all things in being (cf. Colossians 1:16-17). Fr Bede also shows the importance of God's plan in history, while not denying the universal significance of the life, death and resurrection of Jesus Christ.

In concluding this section, I believe that the application of various doctrinal and philosophical insights that come from Hindu philosophy and religion have once again proved extremely valuable in giving new insight into the formulation of the doctrine of Christ. Viewing Christ as the cosmic Person, in the Hindu sense, as *purusha,* gives broader insight into the nature of the person of Christ, as well as his work.

Drawing a distinction between *avatara* and Christian incarnation helps to focus more acutely on the importance of a normative act of salvation in Jesus Christ. Struggling with the notion of Jesus' filial qualification as God helps to cement the notion that the Father truly is *sat,* the source, from which all things come, and the Son is *chit,* the Self-knowledge of the Father. Fr Bede's own words best encapsulate the cosmic significance of the doctrine of the cosmic Christ as it relates to varying cultures and faiths:

> It is true that Rama and Krishna also have a universal meaning, just as Buddha's Enlightenment has a meaning for all humanity. But the life and death and resurrection of Christ have not only a meaning for all, but also an effect on history.... Here history has assumed a universal meaning... an ultimate purpose, in that death, resurrection, ascension, and final glorification (Griffiths 1983:128).

Chapter 5

The contribution of Bede Griffiths' cosmic Christology to spiritual experience and theological discourse.

This section of the book attempts to suggest ways in which Fr Bede's spirituality contributes both to the manner in which Christians live out their spirituality and to our articulation of this lived reality. Spiritual experience, and the articulation of this experience, are two essential elements of his spirituality. The introduction to this book makes the point that it is the man, Bede Griffiths, who makes his spirituality unique and valuable – his spirituality is very certainly a result of who he is as a person. Thus studying the person and his experience can offer some insights into the discipline of Christian spirituality. Because of his pioneering courage, his ability to integrate seemingly contradictory cultures and philosophies, and his strong desire to enliven the faith-life of others through sharing his spiritual experiences, Fr Bede's spirituality has a lot to offer those who are seeking a closer and more meaningful relationship with God and all of God's creation.

The importance of his spirituality will thus be discussed under two categories namely, the contribution of his spirituality to practical spiritual experience and then its contribution to theological discourse.

Spiritual experience

The preceding sections of this book have aimed to discuss aspects of the development and content of Bede Griffiths' cosmic Christology. These sections have sketched the way in which Fr Bede was able to bring together seemingly opposites such as science and religion, and the "personalism of Christianity" and the "nondualism of Hinduism" (Bruteau 1996:xiii) through his life-long spiritual search and theological development. What makes Fr Bede noteworthy as a theologian, even he did not consider himself as a theologian in the strictest sense, is that his theology was formulated through reflection upon spiritual experience. Hence, as chapter two suggested, an essential aspect of any discussion of Fr Bede's spirituality has to deal with more than his writings and talks. It should also attempt, in some way, to understand the person and the unwritten, unspoken, content of his spiritual life.

Chapter two said that Fr Bede, as a westerner, adopted many eastern ideas and concepts in his faith in order to achieve a balance between East and West. On the video "A human search: the life of Fr Bede Griffiths" (1993) one hears numerous corroborations from ashramites and colleagues suggesting that Fr Bede's own life, as a Christian *sannyasi* in India, was a model of the 'marriage of East and West' that he so often talked about. Fr Bede is said to have had a unique way of imparting his spirituality to the whole of a human person, both rationally, through his many writings and lectures, and intuitively through his monastic lifestyle at 'Shantivanam' (Forest of Peace) Ashram. Fr Bede's lived spirituality, which of course included his writings and talks, was able to capture both heart and mind. In this regard His Holiness the Dalai Lama writes of Fr Bede:

> I therefore have much admiration for the life-long work of Father Griffiths for inter-religious understanding, and for helping people open their hearts and minds to gain a sense of peace and utility to further the cause of goodwill among all peoples (in Bruteau 1996:xi).

This section of the book is this more personal and practical, aiming to show in what way Fr Bede's cosmic Christology is able to make a contribution to the lived spiritual life of others.

The importance of a contemplative lifestyle.

From the discussion presented in the preceding chapters it has been shown that Fr Bede's spirituality and faith are predominantly experiential as apposed to being largely speculative. By this it is meant that his theological discourse stems from, and flows back into, his spiritual experience. For him, the symbols and concepts of religion and philosophy are useful tools for expressing the reality of a life lived in consciousness of the Centre, the cosmic Christ. In other words, for Fr Bede, a contemplative lifestyle in which one seeks to deepen one's consciousness of God was much more important than having an articulate and theologically accurate explanation of one's spirituality.

Theology is not an end in itself; rather, it is more precisely a means towards expressing the end. As was pointed out in chapter two, Fr Bede's approach to his spirituality was contemplative in nature from before his arrival in India right up to his death. Furthermore, Fr Bede said that it was this contemplative experience, this consciousness which is beyond "all religion" and "every scripture and creed" (Griffiths 1982:42), that gave him insights into reality as it truly is, and as such allowed him to speak of it to others.

> When the mind in meditation goes beyond images and concepts, beyond reason and will to the ultimate Ground of its consciousness, it experiences itself in this timeless and spaceless unity of Being. The Ultimate is experienced in the depth of the soul, in the substance or Centre of its consciousness, as its own Ground or Source, as its very being or Self (Atman). This is an experience of self-transcendence, which gives an insight into Reality (1982:27).

Thus, for Fr Bede the lived consciousness of the non-duality between creation and Creator, and the experience of the cosmic Christ as the divine person that holds all being in divine existence, were important aspects of his spirituality; resultantly, his theology was an articulation of this spirituality. One may go as far as suggesting that Fr Bede was himself a sign or image of 'the Real'. Or, stated more aptly in the words of James Conner, Fr Bede as a *sannyasi,* truly became a sign of the reality that he is (1996:96).

In relation to Fr Bede's cosmic Christology, it is his experience of the person of Christ that informed and shaped his spiritual life. Chapter three suggested that Fr Bede's experience could be characterised in two ways, or along two horizons, as chapter four suggested: First, his experience of Christ was specific, in that it was an experience of the saving and revealing Christ of Christianity. While some may contest and question this statement, he certainly never saw himself as anything other than a Christian. However, Fr Bede also articulates a second kind of experience of Christ that is much more general in nature. This second kind of experience suggests that Christ is of broader significance than the understanding of Christ in the Christian faith alone, and as such this Christ is of cosmic and universal significance. However, whether general or specific, it was a mystical experience of the person of Christ that drew him beyond the supposed dualities between God and self.

> Jesus was taking us to the point where we go beyond all dualities, and the marvellous expression of it is in the Gospel of St. John: "that they may all be one as Thou, Father, in me and I in Thee, that they may be one in us." Jesus is totally one with the Father and yet he is not the Father. It's a non-dual relationship. It's not one and it's not two. It's the mystery of love. Love is not one, and it's not two… When two people unite in love, they become one, and yet they have their distinction. Jesus and the Father have this total communion in love. And he asks us to become one as he is one with the Father, total oneness in the non-dual being of the Father. That's the Christian calling (Griffiths quoted in Valiaveetil 1997:8).

From what Fr Bede wrote it is clear that his Christology was rooted in a very deep experience of God that is testified to in both the Christian and Hindu traditions. Both of these religious traditions emphasise being taken into God, that is, the breaking down of dualities between 'self' and God. However, where the Christian tradition differs is that it emphasises that this experience of non-duality is fundamentally an experience of the Trinitarian God. Fr Bede speaks of Jesus as a *jivanmukta*, that is, one who is intimately in communion with the Father, so much so that he can say "I and the Father are one" (John 10:30) (for a more detailed discussion of Fr Bede's understanding of Jesus (the Son) in relation to the Father, see chapter four). In this understanding, Jesus is not only communicating his experience of his unique relationship to his Father, that is that Jesus and the Father are one, rather Jesus is also communicating his filial distinction from the Father. Consequently, Jesus maintains his identity, as the Son of the Father, while affirming that it is this filial identity that makes him one with the Father. Fr Bede articulates his conscious experience of the trinity further in asserting that Jesus was only capable of knowing of his identity and relationship with the Father through the work of the Holy Spirit within him. Fr Bede explains:

> … in Jesus that capacity to receive the Spirit of God was without limit; he received that fullness of the gift of the Spirit. In this experience of the Spirit he was able to

> know himself as the Son of God, as sharing in the divine
> nature, as expressing the very Word of God.... In this
> knowledge of himself as Son, he was able to know the
> Father, not in part but in fullness. He knew himself as
> the "only Son", the One who alone knows and expresses
> in fullness the mind of the Father (Griffiths quoted in
> Valiaveetil 1997:8).

Thus, in Jesus we see what God desires for all humanity. Jesus was a particular human person who lived in a particular place, and at a particular time in history. However, his intimate communion with the Father, through the Spirit, reveals his unique identity. Jesus had completely given himself over to the indwelling Spirit and in so doing he had achieved perfection in God. Thus, according to Fr Bede's cosmic Christology, Jesus achieved what every human is meant to discover and be, that is, true identity with, and lack of separation from God, through intimate communion (cf. Griffiths 1983:187-188).

This emphasis from Fr Bede's cosmic Christology thus not only shows Jesus as the aim of the spiritual life, but also shows him as the perfect example thereof. Furthermore, it is valuable in that it challenges Christian spirituality to move beyond an unbalanced emphasis on mere morality (which often seems to characterise contemporary western spiritualities), to mysticism as a valid gauge of spiritual maturity.

The relationship between Creator and creation, and the effects of this relationship for eco-human well-being

Fr Bede's amazing ability to live out, and talk about, the non-duality between creation and Creator is a further notable aspect of his cosmic Christology. Chapter three of this book discussed the largely prevalent mindset in the West that views creation as purely materialistic, without any sense of the sacred or divine (cf. Griffiths 1982:9), while chapter four gave some insight into the mindset of the East that so emphasises the mystical element of reality that it often neglects the physical (cf. Griffiths 1982:180). In this light of these over emphasis, Fr Bede suggests that the East and West need each other in order to survive and flourish. What is required is a balance between the philosophies and spiritualities of both East and West, that is, an ability to identify and deal with concrete human, social and ecological concerns, without disregarding the essential role of the spiritual in true wholeness.

Within this context Fr Bede's organic approach to nature is extremely valuable in that it seeks to overcome the dualities presented in a purely mechanistic model of reality (Griffiths 1989:281). His suggestion is that

> ... we have to learn to see ourselves as part of the physical organism of the universe. We need to develop the sense of the cosmic whole and of a way of relating to the world around us as a living being which sustains and nourishes us and for which we have responsibility. This will give rise to a new understanding of our environment and will put an end to this age of the exploitation of nature (1989:282).

Non-dual consciousness of the cosmic Christ is essential to such a shift. Consciousness of the cosmic Christ not only awakens one to the fact that Christ is the creator and sustainer of all that exists, (that is, the Christ who transcends all of material and created reality), it also awakens one to the reality that Christ is part of the created order through his incarnation into matter. Thus he has sanctified creation through his resurrection, and has taken matter into the Godhead through his ascension. As a result, through Christ the

> ... divine life penetrates history, time ...and then raises history and time ...into a new creation, a new order of being in which these things are not lost, not destroyed, but transfigured (Griffiths 1983:127).

This spiritual insight is not unique, yet the way in which Fr Bede arrives at it gives rise to some fresh and useful insights. Fr Bede's insight into the manner in which the cosmic Christ creates and sustains creation stems both from widely accepted Christian doctrines in this regard and also from his acceptance of the cosmic mystery of the Upanishads.

Fr Bede suggests that the saying *tat tvam asi* "Thou art That" is a key to understanding the way in which mystical union with God changes one's view of all of reality and as a result of that paradigm shift, also changes one's view of the rest of creation. He suggests that this saying, like the saying *aham brahmasmi* "I am Brahman", is often misunderstood because of the influences of western dualism. Certainly it may be considered blasphemous many Christians. The is a real problem in that without a mystical understanding of these sayings, and so too of the reality that they describe, one could quite easily come to this incorrect conclusion by regarding the sayings (and the truth they speak of) as blasphemous. Fr Bede is at pains to point out that even Jesus only calls himself God in a qualified sense (see chapter four for a more detailed discussion this point). While Christians believe that they are created in the image of God (Genesis 1:26), and strive to become more like God (in Christ, Romans 8:29), they still maintain a distinction between themselves as creation and God as transcendent Creator. The third 'mahavakya', or Great Saying, from the Upanishads is *sarvam khalvidam brahman asti* "All this world is Brahman", or "All this world is God". Taking these three sayings literally, without the mystical insight from which they stem, would indeed seem to suggest an understanding of God that is quite different to that contained in the Christian tradition, and even Hinduism. However, Fr Bede notes that what is really being emphasised in these sayings is the truth that "I, in the deepest centre, the ground of my being, am one with Brahman, the source of all creation" (Griffiths 1983:57). Fr Bede's suggested that through progress in the 'new science', and developments in transpersonal studies, the mystical realisation is developed that shows that the source of a person's being, the centre of the person, is contained within that One true Self – contained within God who is the only true self.

> When you say "I am Brahman," *Aham Brahmasmi*, what you are saying is that in the inner depths of my being, beyond my ego, beyond my conscious self, I am one with this inner Spirit which is also the Spirit of the universe. In Christian terms you have discovered yourself in God (Griffiths 1983:60).

Such consciousness is thus an awakening to true a identity that is non-dual in nature. It is important to point out again at this stage that this does not mean that a discovery of one's true identity as being 'one with God' is a loss of individual identity. Fr Bede often used Teilhard de Chardin's notion of 'union that differentiates', and 'unity in distinction', to make the point that true individual identity can only be found in God, the true Source of all identity (cf. Valiaveetil 1997:9). The Indian Christology that Fr Bede developed at Shantivanam is rooted in an experience of God found in both the Hindu and Christian traditions. According to Fr Bede, both of these experiences are ultimately *advaitic* in nature (cf. Valiaveetil 1997:9). However, Fr Bede developed the notion of *advaita,* and the way in which unity differentiates, further than it is presented in Hinduism, by relating it to the Trinitarian experience.

Within the Trinity, as in the world, there is not a simple unity, or monism, where everything is 'melted' into one, and so loses its identity. Rather, in the Trinity there is a unity in distinction. The Son is the principal, and clearest example, of unity in distinction, being fully God, yet distinct as Son. In Jesus we see complete union with the Father, yet it is precisely that union with the Father that gives him his identity as the Son of the Father. In relation to this statement it is important to note that one's true identity is not simply swallowed up by that of the rest of creation. However, while your identity is distinct, and not lost, there is no fundamental duality between your true self and the rest of creation. As shown earlier in chapter three, Fr Bede believed that all of creation is interdependent and interrelated with itself, and then of course also with God, its creator. This idea, along with the notion presented above, serves to further emphasise both unity and distinction in the cosmos. As an aside, it is interesting to note that Fr Bede's first awakening to the mystery of God comes through an experience of God in nature (cf. Griffiths 1979:9-12, see also chapter two). His awareness of the divine in nature remained, and grew within him, throughout his life.

Contemplatives are often criticised for being overly concerned with the interior life at the expense of the world around them. This criticism cannot be applied to Fr Bede since he had the concern of 'eco-human well-being' as a central aim and desire in his spirituality. Before discussing this statement it is necessary to give a brief explanation of the term, 'eco-human well-being'. This phrase was coined by Paul Knitter with reference to social and ecological responsibility and how this responsibility leads to well-being (cf. Knitter 1995). It displays an awareness that 'well-being' is not only a human concern, but that all of creation has a need for wholeness. Because the term encompasses both people and nature, which are interconnected, it will be used in this section of the book to describe Fr Bede's view of the relationship of harmony that must exist within the cosmos.

How can Fr Bede's consciousness of non-duality between creation and creator, stemming from his contemplative spirituality, relate to eco-human well-being? First, his spirituality gives rise to a new experience of the mystery of God and creation. That is, his spirituality in general, and his cosmic Christology in particular, emphasise that: God is not separate from humanity, or any part of creation, and moreover, that the true Self of the human person (*atman*) is not separate from the Self of the rest of the universe (*brahman*). Thus, if I am not separate from creation and Christ the creator and sustainer of all creation (i.e. if there is no objective duality or *dvaita* between my self and the Source from which all created reality stems) and I choose to exploit creation, am I not exploiting myself, and ultimately Christ? The same can be said for human relationships and the structure of society. Any society or system that sets out to exploit others is ultimately exploiting Christ himself. Accordingly, it is proposed that Fr Bede's spirituality gives a very clear motive for striving for eco-human well-being. That motive is the honour Christ, and Christ's creation, of which the true self is an integral part.

Thus, Fr Bede's spirituality gives insight into the value of a spiritual life lived in such a manner as to overcome the dualities that often lead to separation: the kind of separation found in many societies between people and God, people and people, and people and creation. Where such dualities exist the results are most often objectification of the 'other' that results in exploitation and abuse.

In the preceding sections it has been noted on a number of occasions that Fr Bede longed for a balance between East and West, between the contemplative depths of eastern spirituality and the active concern for material reality found in the spirituality of the West. The following quote shows Fr Bede's understanding of how the person and work of Christ affects our material world:

> Jesus therefore was a man, in whom body and soul were pure instruments of the indwelling Spirit. In him the destiny of man has been fulfilled. But this inevitably has an effect on the whole cosmos. The universe is a psychosomatic unity, a space-time continuum in which each part depends on every other part as an integrated whole. Whereas in this universe, as we know it, there is conflict at every level and body and soul are in conflict with one another, in Jesus, this conflict has been

> overcome, body and soul have been restored to unity
> with the Spirit, and a power of unification has been
> released in the world. In this sense we can say that the
> death of Jesus, the free surrender of his life on the cross
> to his Father, was a cosmic event (1983:187-188).

Thus, as pointed out in chapter four, the soteriological significance of Christ reaches to all levels of the cosmos, and not just to human persons as much contemporary Christian theology seems to suggest. Moreover, one can further say that in a universe in which each part depends upon every other part – a universe that is still evolving towards true Christ consciousness – any activity that exploits creation in any way stunts God's goal for the evolutionary process. As one's unity with Christ grows more and more, one is able to overcome the conflicts that wreak havoc in creation and in so doing move closer to the destiny of all humanity, that is, blissful unity with God and creation.

No doubt there are many other points that could be made in order to extrapolate emphases in Fr Bede's spirituality that can be of use for an authentic, lived, spirituality. However, the two suggestions above are merely two examples, showing ways in which Fr Bede's cosmic Christology can contribute towards a lived spirituality. The rest of this chapter will highlight some ways in which Fr Bede's Christology can contribute to theological discourse and the discipline of Christology within Christian doctrine.

Theological discourse

Many theologians[23] are becoming increasingly aware that speculative reason and philosophical discourse are limited sources for discovering and expressing the revelation and will of God (cf. Schneiders 1990:17). There are an increasing number of theologians who are of the mind that spirituality serves as an essential source for the development and furtherance of true systematic theologies. In short, theologians from various theological perspectives (whether they be feminist, African, Liberation, or contextual theologians) are suggesting that the speculative and philosophical questions of previous ages are not sufficient to deal with the real human need for discovery and engagement with God's revelation. The sections that follow show how Fr Bede's spirituality is able to make a valuable contribution to the way

in which we 'do theology' that stems from a lived spiritual experience
– thus it will consider some issues in theological methodology.

Theological methodology

This book has already made the point a number of times, that Fr Bede's
spirituality is primarily a spirituality based on mystical experience of
God. It needs to be kept in mind that he was first and foremost a monk,
and thus only a theologian by virtue of the fact that he desired to share
his experiences with others. In order to do so he had to articulate them
in theological language and symbols. Yet, it is precisely because of this
experiential emphasis that his spirituality can offer valuable insights
into the process of doing sound theology.

The effects of the spiritual awakening in contemporary society
(that is often not directly associated with any one religion or faith
tradition) cannot be ignored. This quest for truth and meaning is
traversing a variety of disciplines, and is making an impact upon
the sciences, social sciences and many other related fields. Whereas
in the past any form of subjectivity within the sciences was frowned
upon, there is an increasing awareness that the subject is intimately
involved in, and radically affects, the process of discovery[24]. While
this recognition is not solely as a result of the greater spiritual
awakening that is taking place in the West, the principles that
underpin such approaches are often strikingly similar to those
expressed in spirituality. Moreover, there is no doubt that where this
awakening is taking place, it has had a marked affect academic
methodology in various disciplines. In theology in particular, the
role of human experience is no longer discounted when it comes to
the formulation of orthodox doctrine.

A number of theologians, notable amongst them being Raimundo
Panikkar, Gustavo Guitierrez, and Ewert Cousins, are affirming
spiritual and existential experience as a primary source of theological
formulation. Cousins writes about his own theological methodology
that,

> In a basic way, spirituality is experiential; it is bound up
> with praxis, specifically orthopraxis. As such it should
> provide material for theological reflection. At the same
> time spirituality should be enriched and guided by

> theology. I [view]... spirituality as experience... and
> theology as reflection upon experience (1992:59).

In a similar way Fr Bede has offered a great deal of insight into the
importance of experience and reflection thereon, which forms the basis
for articulation of the experience in theological terms. In summary, he
showed, through his own methodology how to move from spirituality
to theology. Within the context of Fr Bede's cosmic Christology, and
his emphasis on the universal significance of the person and work of
Christ, such an experiential methodology is extremely valuable.

One can cite Panikkar's thoughts on inter-religious encounter as an
example of why a methodology of orthopraxis is valuable and
necessary in a pluralistic context. Panikkar suggests that a theological
methodology based on experience and praxis is the only way in which
claims of the universal significance of Christ will be considered by a
non-Christian. His argument is based on the fact that inter-religious
dialogue has often failed because it has sought to start with discourse
and theological dialogue. When persons from different religions meet
to dialogue theologically they are discussing philosophical concepts,
religious symbols and cultural associations. This process is mediated
through a particular understanding of the meanings of these symbols
and concepts and can often be hindered by a lack of an adequate
symbolic or linguistic vocabulary that is able to bring together
differing cultural and social understandings of the terms and images
being used. Surely, we would agree that language and symbol are only
representative expressions of the true reality around which such
encounters should be based? It is the truth, the experience itself, the
reality that one is seeking to express, that is of much higher
importance. As such Panikkar asserts that the only place that true
encounter can take place between religions, and even cultures, is at the
place where they truly meet. He suggests that place is an experience of
the unknown or universal Christ that is present in all true religion
(1988:126). Within the context of Christianity and Hinduism he writes
the following:

> Christianity and Hinduism both meet in Christ. Christ is
> their meeting point... we cannot 'prove' this statement
> rationally. We can only try to show ...that they do not
> meet at any other point... the true meeting point of
> religions does not belong to the essential, but to the

> existential sphere. Religions may meet in my heart, and
> not in my ideas (Panikkar 1988:127-132).

The point of the above quotation is simply to illustrate the necessity of
spiritual experience as a starting point for theological discourse. It is
not my intention to grapple with Panikkar's views on the relationship
between Christianity and Hinduism. Rather, all that needs to be noted
is that Panikkar's assertion on the validity of spiritual experience is
very similar to Fr Bede's own views. This is not surprising since they
were colleagues and spent a good deal of time together in India.
Panikkar affirms that religions cannot truly hope to meet through
discourse or reason, neither in concepts of God, but only *in* God.
Everything in existence exists within God. However, as Fr Bede asserts
many times, the link between God and all things is Christ from whom
all things come and in whom all things subsist (cf. Griffiths 1983:75;
1989:118-127). It is from this common experience of the mystery of
the Absolute, from different backgrounds and traditions, that one can
begin to formulate and articulate a more accurate an inclusive theology.

Abhishiktananda, a precursor of Fr Bede (see chapter two), who
also emphasised the primacy of spiritual experience, sums up this view
very clearly when he writes:

> India's secret will be transmitted in the Church only very
> secondarily by means of the word, writing or university
> teaching. Rather, what is at issue here is more like an
> ontological transmission, from depth to depth, soul to
> soul, in the great silence. Words and writings do not
> reach to the *depths* unless they already spring from the
> depths of the individual from whom they issue
> (1983:72-73).

What is important to note is that within such an understanding of
theology there is an attempt to move beyond what is located in the
intellect. In other words, there is a realisation that the human mind
could never fully capture the mystery of God in Christ, and that sound
theological methodology needs to be open to the fact that speculative
and reasoned outcome will always fall short of the reality it is
attempting to describe.

> Faith has to do with what cannot be seen. But even
> though faith is located in the intellect, it far surpasses it;
> and the intellect, even when enlightened by grace, is

> unable to comprehend the whole mystery.... It is
> precisely in transcending even the highest reach of the
> human mind, in passing beyond all symbols and
> expressions of itself, that faith reveals itself in its
> essential purity. This is the essential "void" in which
> alone the human person is open to and able to hear the
> eternal Word (Abhishiktananda 1984 a:199).

While Fr Bede's contemplative desire was not as intense as that of
Abhishiktananda, he still adhered to the same principles of passing
beyond words and symbols in order to move closer to the truth. Fr
Bede's approach did however have an integrative aspect to it in which
he emphasised that one does not reject what one transcends rather one
integrates it as one transcends it (cf. Griffiths 1982:42-43; 1983:53-61,
and the analogous discussion of how letters integrate into words, and
words into sentences, and sentences into books to create greater
meaning – chapter two).

The key benefits of such a theological approach are twofold. First,
such an approach recognises the fact that ultimately all theology is
mediated through the experiences of human persons in relation to a
transcendent Reality – God reveals God's self, and our experience of
God is mediated through who and what we are. Second, this method of
theology recognises as a basic premise that language and concepts can
never fully contain or explain the mystery of God. It is here that I
believe Fr Bede's theological approach is particularly valuable, not
only for theology in general, but particularly for interfaith encounter.
This humble awareness creates a new openness to relating, and
discovering, truth in cultural and religious contexts that are often
radically different in their underlying theology and philosophy. This
point leads to the next significant contribution that Fr Bede's cosmic
Christology has to offer to theological methodology and discourse.

Theological language employed in formulating doctrine

The previous section maintains that experiences of Reality need to be
communicated through the use of language and concepts. Traditionally
the Christian faith has attempted to explain its truths through the
language of the Christian scriptures, interpreting and expounding the
scriptures through the lens of the tradition and symbols of the church
(e.g., the Patristics which are inextricably linked to the philosophy of

the Greek Fathers as expressed in the language of Plato and Aristotle). However, as is pointed out in chapters two and four, there is a growing realisation that for the Christian faith to be universally acceptable it needs to have an open dialogue with the cultures, philosophies, concepts, and religions of the rest of the world, not just those which are informed by the ancient Greek and Latin cultures and languages. Fr Bede suggests that,

> Christianity no less than the other religions of the world is required to undergo a death and resurrection, if it is to enter into genuine dialogue with other religious traditions and become adapted to Asia and Africa (1984:222).

Sadly this death is coming to pass as faith in western society becomes less and less prominent. Fr Bede's cosmic Christology is very valuable in this regard in that it illustrates how he draws not only from the richness of the language used throughout the history of the Christian tradition (predominantly adopted from the Christian West), but also from the vast treasures of the language and philosophy found in the religions and cultures of the East (cf. Griffiths 1983:76). There is a sense in which one could say that his traditional Christian roots, as found in the Catholic Church, had to undergo a death when he left England, and were reborn over the years he spent in India (see chapter two).

Clearly, Fr Bede's approach, that seeks to inculturate the Christian faith through encounter and dialogue with the religions of the East, would prove valuable in many other contexts, such as Africa, Asia, and even some post Christian western societies. Encounter and dialogue with other religions in this context refers not only to a superficial encounter and dialogue, but rather to a mystical encounter that goes beyond the doctrines and philosophies of the particular faiths concerned, to the reality they seek to express and represent. From this common mystical experience of true unity, authentic dialogue and mutual enrichment can flow (see the discussion in the previous section). Thus, Fr Bede's 'marriage of East and West' is valuable in terms of religious, philosophical, and cultural reciprocity. Moreover it highlights the subsequent linguistic and conceptual categories that can be added to the Christian faith in order to help the faith, and its doctrines, to be born into new and different theological contexts. There is another element that must be mentioned, current trends show that Christianity faces an added challenge of seeking to discover and articulate a fuller truth through encounter with people of other faiths. Stated simply, the missionary arrogance of the 18th and 19th century, that assumed that God only revealed God's self and God's will through the Christian West, has been found to be false. Fr Bede writes:

> It is no longer possible today for one religion to live in isolation from other religions. For many this presents a real problem. Each religion has been taught to regard itself as the one true religion and to reject all other religions as false, so that to enter into dialogue with other religions is not easy.... We begin to realise that truth is one, but that it has many faces, and each religion is, as it were, a face of the one Truth, which manifests itself under different signs and symbols in the different historical traditions (1982:25).

Thus, Fr Bede affirms that true encounter and dialogue can be valuable as a means through which one can come to a fuller understanding of the truth about God and reality, both of which transcend the categories and forms that we tend to attach to them in our various religions. In the face of a myriad of truths, one's absolutes tend to become relative, and one discovers greater truths and a more effective language and symbolic system through which to communicate them. Fr Bede's own spiritual experience is a prime example of how inter-religious encounter can enrich one's theological vocabulary through an exposure to a vast array of "different signs and symbols" – such as the doctrine of *purusha* that Fr Bede adapted to Christianity through his encounter with Hinduism (see chapter four).

Conclusion

Fr Bede is regarded by many as a spiritual pioneer (cf. du Boulay 1998:288). Rajan puts this point across so well in using the metaphor of an explorer. He writes:

> Swami Bede is a sannyasin engaged in space exploration! In this technological age when the scientists are engaged in exploring the outer space, Swami Bede is engaged in exploring the inner space, the space within his own heart (Rajan 1989:114).

Just as explorers in outer space have much to offer from their discoveries in un-chartered 'outer space', so too Fr Bede has a great deal to offer from his explorations in 'inner space'. This section has shown how Fr Bede's experiential, and mystical, spirituality affirms and enriches the views of many theologians who maintain that true theology can only stem from a mystical experience of the God who reveals the content of theology. This section also argued that such experience transcends one particular religion or culture, yet it can be transferred into, and expressed through, the language and concepts of many cultures in order to give a broader and more meaningful expression of the ultimately inexpressible truth.

Chapter 6

Final thoughts and further steps

What we've covered in this book.

This book has investigated aspects of Fr Bede Griffiths' cosmic Christology as they arise from his spirituality. The basic approach has been that his cosmic Christology is insightful and valuable because it stemmed from his spiritual experiences as a sannyasi in India.

First, there was a discussion on some significant events and experiences in Fr Bede's life, showing how these influenced and developed his spirituality. The finding of this section of the book was that Fr Bede, as a Christian sannyasi, sought to move beyond language, sacred texts, rituals and concepts of faith, (particularly those that are commonplace in western Christianity), in order to gain a mystical experience of God – who is ultimately beyond names and forms. Having experienced the cosmic Christ as the source, sustainer, and goal of all creation, he desired to share his discovery with both Christians and Hindus. In order to express the mystery of the cosmic Christ that he had experienced, Fr Bede relied on new concepts and language that came from the theologies of Christianity in India, and the Hindu religion. In particular, he expressed his cosmic Christology by drawing on three areas of philosophy and theology. First, his Christology was informed by his understanding of God's revelation. These insights came from both eastern and western understandings of revelation. Second, it was informed by his understanding and experience of reality as being physical, psychological and spiritual. This area of his thought was strongly influenced by the Hindu understanding of reality. Thirdly, it was informed by insights he gained from the 'new scientific' paradigm, particularly drawing upon selected aspects of quantum theory, biology, transpersonal psychology and the perennial philosophy. His mystical experience was corroborated by scientific advances and discoveries being made in the West at that stage. One of the notable findings in this section was Fr Bede's desire to have East and West complement each other by overcoming the deficiencies in their respective word-views. The next step in the argument presented aspects of Fr Bede's cosmic Christology that were innovative and useful. They were felt to be of value since they illustrated the way in which Fr Bede drew upon traditional Christian theology, as well as on innovative expressions of the cosmic Christ that arise from his contact with Hinduism, in order to express his experience of the cosmic Christ more completely and accurately. The primary finding of this section was that Fr Bede's cosmic Christology found expression on two 'horizons' or levels. First, he spoke of Christ in Christian terms, drawing upon the traditional doctrine of the cosmic Christ, constantly showing the unique and special revelatory relationship that Christ had to the Christian faith throughout its history. However, he also sought to express the idea that the cosmic Christ has a much broader significance than one religion. In essence Christ existed and was active long before the advent of the Christian faith. In articulating this aspect of his Christology he drew upon the theology of the cosmic Person as found in Hinduism. Having discussed the manner in which Fr Bede expressed his experience of the cosmic Christ, the argument concluded with a discussion of the significance of Fr Bede's cosmic Christology for developing a methodology of theological encounter that can overcome the deficiencies of mere dialogue.

In addition to the above, it needs to be noted that what makes Fr Bede's spirituality so significant is the way in which he lived and embodied the spiritual ideals that he taught.

In 1993 Fr Bede was given the John Harriott award for outstanding work in religious communication. Sadly, du Boulay records in her biography that Fr Bede did not feel that he had fully succeeded in conveying his message (1998:288). Many of those who knew him personally would consider Fr Bede's judgement of himself too stringent. His teaching and example have changed numerous lives, and communities, bringing a fresh and vibrant content and approach to the experience of God in Christ.

His life and spirituality were groundbreaking in many regards, and on many occasions ahead of their time. The 'National Catholic Reporter' wrote: "Even at age 86 and on the edge of death, Benedictine Fr Bede Griffiths was still running so far ahead of the pack that his life's momentum will quicken him for many springs to come" (quoted in du Boulay 1998:288). Many conservatives, both Christians and Hindus, have been critical of Fr Bede's lifestyle and teaching – such criticism should naturally be considered if one is to be open and honest. On the other hand, many less conservative Christians and Hindus regard him as "one of the great religious prophets of modern times" (du Boulay 1998:288). I believe that the Camaldolese official statement after Fr Bede's death best sums up why his life and spirituality are able to offer so much to contemporary Christian spirituality:

> The radiance of his personal presence was the best commentary on his theories of interfaith relations... he was an example of the practice of interfaith dialogue and study as a way of realizing the highest Christian ideals of holiness and of mystical union with God (in du Boulay 1998:289).

His lived example of an integrated spirituality of East and West is even more significant when one considers it in the light of Karl Rahner's assertion which was quoted in the introduction to this book: "the Christian of the future will be a mystic or he or she will not exist at all" (quoted in Schneiders 1990:677).

It is in this regard that Fr Bede's cosmic Christology has so much to offer.

In a world of increasing pluralism where information and ideas are so easily shared, where contact between differing cultures and religions is becoming far more frequent, there is bound to be significant change to both Christian doctrine and spirituality. Here Fr Bede's cosmic Christology serves as a good example of how one can enrich and develop one's own spirituality and theology by integrating different religious and cultural paradigms (cf. chapters three and four). Raimundo Panikkar, in his tribute to Fr Bede, suggests that it was Fr Bede's person, and particularly his tolerance and vision that helped him to formulate such a well balanced spirituality. Panikkar encourages his readers to use Fr Bede's spirituality as a sound basis upon which we can "go forward and take our own further steps into the future" (1996:33)

Where can we go from here? Some further steps.

So, what are some possible further steps that can be taken? First, as is shown above, there is a need to follow Fr Bede's example of living out an integrated, and contextually honest, spirituality. There is little doubt that such integrity is costly and requires great valour. As has already been mentioned in this section, many were critical of the way in which he transcended the normative boundaries of Christianity and Hinduism (cf. du Boulay 1998:292). Regardless of this, through his spirituality, Fr Bede showed the wonderful depth of insight that can be gained when one is prepared to challenge accepted norms in the quest for a greater truth. The truth that he sought, as illustrated in his cosmic Christology, is beyond the confines of a single culture, philosophy, or religion. It is a truth that is of universal significance and value. Venturing into such relatively uncharted Christian spiritual territory takes courage, yet it is worthwhile. It is this kind of courage that is required of those of us who are to take further steps in following Fr Bede's example.

Next, there is the important step of building on the example of Fr Bede's inculturated spirituality. This is particularly valuable in areas where faith has tended to run alongside, or in opposition to, indigenous culture (such as Christianity in Africa and South America). If the Gospel is to have global significance there is an urgency for its proponents to engage honestly with the culture into which it is entering, or have entered. As societies mature, and the shackles of colonialism and imperialism are loosed, those Christian communities that have not found a way of respecting, understanding, and integrating, the valuable elements of their culture and context will simply be rejected as outdated relics of a bygone era. Accordingly, Fr Bede realised that the Gospel would only have significance and efficacy in the life of the Hindu person if it was made more acceptable to the Hindu way of life.

> The Church remains cut off by all its habits of thought from those deep sources of spiritual life and thought which have moulded the character of the Indian people for four thousand years. Unless some means is found of making contact with these sources, there seems to be absolutely no hope (except by a miracle of grace which we have no right to expect) of Christianity making any deep impression on the mind of India (Griffiths 1984:89).

The courage to engage honestly with other cultures should be applied to Christianity in places such as Africa, South America, Asia, and many other areas of the world where western culture and religion may seem foreign. What is required is a reciprocity of cultures and a critical evaluation of both positive and negative aspects of the generally accepted 'cultural packaging' of Christianity in relation to the culture with which it is engaging – the key here is an open, respectful, encounter. Fr Bede writes of his own experience of this process of inculturation in India saying,

> It is in this witness to Christ, through a life lived in intimate union with him, which we believe to be the work of the monk in India today. Ultimately, a Hindu will not be convinced by arguments, but by a life in the closest intimacy with God (1984:47).

Such sincerity is exemplary to the contemporary Christian who seeks to live out an honest and culturally sensitive faith.

As final step for now, and as an encouragement, I would like to highlight the manner in which Fr Bede drew on a wide range of disciplines in order to enrich his spirituality and increase his ability to accurately express and articulate his experience. Of particular importance is the way in which Fr Bede's spirituality has been used as a springboard for the bridging of the gulf between science and religion by many who had long since given up on faith in favour of the 'hard facts' of science. Of late there has been a great deal of research in the area of the interface between science and spirituality. Fr Bede was one of the pioneers in this area, long before it was popular to study it. However, there is a great deal more to be discovered such discoveries can only enrich both science and religion and further stimulate discussion and positive encounter.

What I suggest here are merely three 'further steps' among many that I believe can arise from the example of Fr Bede's spirituality as seen in his cosmic Christology. The three are: the courage to seek the truth, the desire to be enriched through encounter with different cultures and religions, and an engagement with a wide array of disciplines outside of traditional theology. I am sure that there are many brighter minds, and more committed hearts, that will find meaningful and helpful further steps to suggest beyond these three.

Shirley du Boulay pays a fitting tribute to the contribution that Fr Bede's spirituality has already made in the lives of many. This quote is a fitting conclusion, showing the true significance of Fr Bede's cosmic Christology, as it arises from his spirituality.

> Bede's vision was for all humankind, but it is of special importance to Christians. Through his own great longing to reach the reality beyond the opposites, the mystical union that he was convinced lay at the heart of every religion, he helped today's Christian to realise that it is possible to follow a mystical path and remain within the institutional church. In his humility and confidence of the truth of his experience he challenged the Church and left an image of an inclusive Christian for the future, once more his own example, his courage, inspiring others to follow his instincts.... He was like yeast, leavening the flour and water of institutional religion, seeing its point of transcendence where all is one and where all is love. In his life and thought, Bede Griffiths eventually found the meeting place between the opposites. His whole life and thought culminated in the knowledge that beyond the opposites, beyond the darkness, was 'that Great Person, of the brightness of the sun' (1998:292).

Appendix A

A glossary of Sanskrit terms

Term	Explanation
acharya	teacher. Often the head of an ashram.
advaita	non-duality
aham brahmamsi	I am Brahman (God)
ananda (ānanda)	pure joy, bliss
ariti	waving of lights and incense
ashram	abode of ascetics, place of spiritual work
ashrama	stage of life, stages of the spiritual journey
atman	God within each person, Spirit
atyesthi	death ceremony
avatara	incarnation, descent
avidya	ignorance
brahmachari	moving in Brahman, a student
brahman	the Absolute, God
brahmavidya	knowledge of God
bhakti	devotion
bhakti marga	the way of devotion
chit (cit)	consciousness
darshanas	philosophies
devas	shining ones, gods
dharma	the law of life
diksa	ceremony of initiation
dvaita	duality
grhastha	householder
jivanmukta	one who has attained liberation during his lifetime. A person who is one with God

Term	Explanation
jivatman	individual soul
jnana marga	the way of knowledge
karma	action, work
karmamarga	the way of work
lila	the play of God, God's purposeful activity in the world
mantra	prayer or sacred word
maya	creative power, magic, illusion
moksa	final liberation, salvation
murti	image or form
nirguna brahman	God without attributes
om	the sacred syllable, symbol of Brahman, the creative word
purusha	man, cosmic Man, cosmic Person, archetypal Person
sannyasa diksha	the ritual initiation into sannyasa
sannyasi	a monk
sat	being
shakti	the power of God
shanti	peace
shantivanam	forest of peace
shiva	name of God, the destroyer and regenerator
tapas	self control, penance
vanaprastha	forest hermit
veda	knowledge, sacred scripture
vedanta	the end of the Vedas, philosophy
vishnu	name of God, the preserver

(Based on glossaries of terms in Griffiths 1983:133-136 and Rajan 1989:275-280).

Select Bibliography

General

Abhishiktananda 1983. *The eyes of light.* New Jersey: Dimension Publishers.

Abhishiktananda 1984. *The further shore: Three essays by Abhishiktananda.* Delhi: Indian SPCK.

Berky, RF Edwards, SA (edd.) 1993. *Christology in dialogue.* Ohio: The Pilgrim Press.

Bohm, D 1980. *Wholeness and the implicate order.* Routledge: Kegan Paul Publishers.

Bohm, D 1993. Science, spirituality, and the present world crisis. *Revision* Vol. 15 No. 4.

Bruteau, B 1990. Freedom: If anyone is in Christ that person is a new creation. *Who do people say that I am?* (Edd. Eigo F.A and Fittipaldi S.E) Philadelphia: Villanova University Press.

Bruteau, B (ed.) 1996. *The other half of my soul: Bede Griffiths and the Hindu–Christian dialogue.* Wheaton IL: Quest Books.

Capra, F Steindl-Rast, D (edd.) 1991. *Belonging to the universe: Explorations on the frontiers of science and spirituality.* San Francisco: Harper Collins.

Conner, J 1996. The monk as a bridge between East and West. *The other half of my soul: Bede Griffiths and the Hindu–Christian dialogue.* (Ed. Bruteau). Wheaton IL: Quest Books.

Cousins, EH 1990. What is Christian spirituality? *Modern Christian spirituality.* (Ed. Hanson, B). Atlanta: Scholars Press.

Cousins, EH 1992. *Christ of the 21st century.* Brisbane: Element.

Du Boulay, S 1998. *Beyond the darkness: A biography of Bede Griffiths.* London: Rider Books.

Eire, CMN 1990. Major problems in the definition of spirituality as an academic discipline. *Modern Christian spirituality.* (Ed. Hanson, B). Atlanta: Scholars Press.

Forster, DA 2005. Post-human Consciousness and the Evolutionary Cosmology of Pierre Teilhard de Chardin, in *Grace and Truth – a journal of Catholic reflection for Southern Africa.* Volume 22, No 2, August 2005, pp. 29-44.

Forster, DA 2006a. *Validation of individual consciousness in strong artificial intelligence: An African theological contribution.* Pretoria. D.Th Thesis. University of South Africa.

Forster, DA 2006. Identity in relationship: The ethics of ubuntu as an answer to the impasse of individual consciousness. In *The impact of knowledge systems on human development in Africa"* du Toit, CW (ed) 2006. Pretoria. Research institute for Theology and Religion, University of South Africa.

Fox, M 1988. *The coming of the cosmic Christ : The healing of Mother Earth and the birth of a global renaissance.* San Francisco: Harper Collins.

Gaybba, BP 1981. Vatican II's approach to non-Christian religions. *Christianity among the religions.* (Ed. Vorster, WS). Pretoria: UNISA.

Griffiths, B 1966. *Christian ashram: Essays towards a Hindu-Christian dialogue.* London: Darton, Longman & Todd.

Griffiths, B 1976. *Return to the centre.* London: Collins.

Griffiths, B 1979. *The golden string.* London: Harper Collins.

Griffiths, B 1982. *The marriage of East and West: A sequel to the golden string*. London: Collins.

Griffiths, B 1983. *The cosmic revelation: The Hindu way to God*. London: Collins.

Griffiths, B 1984. *Christ in India: Essays towards a Hindu-Christian dialogue*. Springfield: Template Publishers.

Griffiths, B 1987. *River of compassion: A Christian commentary on the Bhagavad Gita*. New York: Amity House.

Griffiths, B 1990. *A new vision of reality: Western science, eastern mysticism and Christian faith*. F Edwards (ed). London: Collins.

Griffiths, B 1992. *The new creation in Christ*. London: Longman and Todd.

Griffiths, B 1995. *Pathways to the Supreme: The personal notebook of Bede Griffiths*. (Ed. Ropers, RR). London: HarperCollins Publishers.

Griffiths, B Sethna, KD 1996. *A follower of Christ and a disciple of Sri Aurobindo: Correspondence between Bede Griffiths and K D Sethna (Amil Kiran)*. Waterford: The Integral Life Foundation.

Grof, S 1984. *Ancient wisdom and modern science*. London: SUNY Press.

Gutierrez, G 1988. *A theology of liberation*. London: SCM Press.

Hale, R 2000. Teilhard de Chardin and Bede Griffiths. *The golden string: Bulletin of the Bede Griffiths Trust* Vol. 7 No. 2.

Hanson, BC 1990. Spirituality as spiritual theology. *Modern Christian spirituality*. (Ed. Hanson, B). Atlanta: Scholars Press.

Hanson, BC (ed.) 1990. *Modern Christian spirituality*. Atlanta. Scholars Press.

Keepin, W 1993. Lifework of David Bohm: River of truth. *Revision* Vol. 16 No. 1.

Knitter, PF 1995. *One earth many religions: Multi-faith dialogue & global responsibility.* New York: Orbis Books.

Link, HG (ed.) 1988. *One God, one Lord, one Spirit: An explication of the apostolic faith today.* Geneva: World Council of Churches Publications.

Lyons, JA 1982. *The Cosmic Christ in Origen and Teilhard de Chardin.* Oxford: Oxford University Press.

Martin, J 1997. Who do you say that I am? *The golden string: Bulletin of the Bede Griffiths Trust* Vol. 4 No. 2.

Panikkar, R 1988. The unknown Christ of Hinduism. *Christianity and other religions.* (Edd. Hick, J and Hebblethwaite, B). Philadelphia: Fortress Press.

Panikkar, R 1996. A tribute. *The other half of my soul: Bede Griffiths and the Hindu–Christian dialogue* (Ed. Bruteau, B). Wheaton IL: Quest Books.

Rajan, J 1989. *Bede Griffiths and sannyasa.* Bangalore: Asian Trading Corporation Publications.

Russell, RJ 1985. The physics of David Bohm and its relevance to philosophy and theology. *Zygon* Vol. 20 No. 2.

Schneiders, SM 1990. Spirituality in the academy. *Modern Christian spirituality.* (Ed. Hanson, B). Atlanta: Scholars Press.

Sharpe, KJ 1990. Relating the physics and religion of David Bohm. *Zygon* Vol. 25 No. 1.

Sharpe, KJ 1993. Holomovement metaphysics and theology. *Zygon* Vol. 28 No. 1.

Sheldrake, R 1996. Mysticism and the new science. *The other half of my soul: Bede Griffiths and the Hindu–Christian dialogue* (Ed. Bruteau, B). Wheaton: Quest Books.

Snyman, K 2002. *Myth, mind, Messiah: Exploring the development of the Christian responsibility toward interfaith dialogue from within Ken Wilber's integral hermeneutics.* Pretoria. D.Th Thesis. University of South Africa.

Spink, K 1988. *A sense of the sacred: A biography of Bede Griffiths*. London: SPCK.

Talbot, M 1991. *The holographic universe*. London: HarperCollins Publishers.

Teasdale, W 1996. Towards a cosmic theology. *The golden string: Bulletin of the Bede Griffiths Trust* Vol. 3 No. 2.

Teilhard de Chardin, P 1965. *Science and Christ*. London: Collins.

Teilhard de Chardin, P 1974. *The future of man*. London: Collins.

Valiaveetil, C 1997. An Indian Christology: The Shantivanam school. *The golden string: Bulletin of the Bede Griffiths Trust* Vol. 4 No. 2.

Vattakuzhy, E 1981. *Indian Christian sannyasa and Swami Abhishiktananda*. Banglore: Theological Publications in India.

Wilber, K 1975. Psychologia perennis: The spectrum of consciousness. *Journal of Transpersonal Psychology* Vol 7 No. 2.

Wilber, K 1979. *No boundary: Eastern and western approaches to personal growth*. California: Center Publications.

Wong, J 1996. Jesus Christ in Bede Griffiths' Christian-Hindu dialogue. *The golden string: Bulletin of the Bede Griffiths Trust* Vol. 3 No. 2.

Videos

A human search: the life of Fr Bede Griffiths. 1993. MTI Films.

Bede Griffiths: interview with Sam Keen. 1990. Spiritual Renaissance Project.

The space in the heart of the lotus: Bede Griffiths a Benedictine in India. 1993. MTI Films.

Web sites and electronic articles

The Bede Griffiths web site: http://www.bedegriffiths.com

The Christopher Dawson centre of Christian culture: http://members.nbci.com/cdawson.htm

The Advaita-Vedanta home page: http:// www.advaita-vedanta.org/

Davies, P 2000. Quantum Computing: The Key to Ultimate Reality? http://www.science-spirit.org

Judith, A 1996. Sri Aurobindo. http://www.gaiamind.org

Index

Endnotes

[1] For an excellent biographical synopsis of Fr Bede's life see the article by Sr. Pascaline Coff O.S.B at http://www.bedegriffiths.com/bio.htm .

[2] C.S. Lewis and Fr Bede struck up a lasting friendship during Fr Bede's time at Oxford. Over the years they corresponded with each other on many occasions. Both Spink (1988) and du Boulay (1998) refer to this friendship and the effect it had on Fr Bede's life and spiritual development. Please do read their excellent books for more detailed information on this significant relationship.

[3] Christopher Dawson (1889-1970) was an Oxford-educated historian and a Catholic in faith. He was author of such works as: The Age of the Gods (1927); Progress and Religion (1929); Enquiries into Religion and Culture (1933); Religion and the Modern State (1935) and Beyond Politics (1939) (cf. http://members.nbci.com/dawson.htm).

[4] Abhishiktananda, previously known as Dom Henri le Saux, was a co-founder of Shantivanam Ashram (together with Fr Jules Monchanin). Abhishiktananda was far more deeply attracted to the advaitic ideals of Hindu mysticism than Fr Bede. While Abhishiktananda and Fr Bede did not always agree on the manner of the relationship between Christianity and Hinduism, and particularly the mystical life, Fr Bede was significantly influenced by Abhishiktananda both through his person and his prolific writings. Abhishiktananda left Shantivanam before Fr Bede's arrival in order to deepen his mystical spirituality. I have written an article on Abhishiktananda, that is yet unpublished. If you're interested in this synopsis of his life and spirituality please feel free to contact me for a copy (my details can be found at the end of the acknowledgements).

[5] It will be shown in the section that follows that this aspect of Fr Bede's spirituality stems from his life as a sannyasi.

[6] The details of this particular aspect will be presented in chapters three and four.

[7] This book only points out specific areas in which Fr Bede's Christology was influenced by the work of Pierre Teilhard de Chardin. For a succinct examination of the overall impact that Teilhard's theology had on Fr Bede's theology see: Hale, R 2000. "Teilhard de Chardin and Bede Griffiths". *The golden string: Bulletin of the Bede Griffiths Trust* Vol. 7 No. 2.

[8] As will be seen further in chapter two, Fr Bede found a great affinity between his view of reality and that of David Bohm, the quantum physicist. Bohm wrote, "The entire universe is basically a single,

indivisible... but flexible and ever changing, unit" (Bohm in Russell 1985:135, see also Bohm 1980 and 1993, Keepin 1993).

[9] Along with Bohm 1980, see also Keepin 1993 and Talbot 1991:43-48 for a more detailed discussion of Bohm's theory of the implicate and explicate orders. The intricate technical details of this view are not a necessary component in furthering the argument that Fr Bede finds this view of reality more acceptable than the Newtonian/Cartesian world-view. All that is necessary to note at this point is that Bohm's view overcomes the imposed dualities on matter that arise from reductionist science and metaphysics.

[10] Ken Wilber has made some significant, and truly remarkable, amendments to his early notion of the 'pluridimensional' model of consciousness. In particular his work in relation to the all quadrant, all level (AQAL), model of consciousness is worth studying. For a detailed discussion of this please see chapter 4 of Forster 2006a, and pages 70-101 of Snyman 2002. However, most of these developments in Wilber's work only took place after Fr Bede's death, and so they do not relate directly to Fr Bede's understanding of reality and consciousness.

[11] A discussion of the concept of "Unity that differentiates" in relation to Fr Bede's Christology will take place in chapter five.

[12] While Fr Bede would not have been aware of developments in 'Quantum computing', there have been some significant advances in this area of late. Of particular interest to this research is the notion of interdependence and interconnectivity that is gaining greater acceptance. Paul Davies writes concerning a comment by David Deutsch:

> A quantum computer, by its very logical nature, is in principle capable of simulating the entire quantum universe in which it is embedded. It is therefore the ultimate virtual reality machine. In other words, a small part of reality can in some sense capture and embody the whole. The fact that the physical universe is constructed in this way – that wholes and parts are mutually enfolded in mathematical self-consistency – is a stunning discovery that impacts on philosophy and even theology. By achieving quantum computation, mankind will lift a tiny corner of the veil of mystery that shrouds the ultimate nature of reality. We shall finally have captured the vision elucidated so eloquently by William Blake more than centuries ago:

To see a World in a grain of sand, And a Heaven in a wild flower, Hold infinity in the palm of your hand, And eternity in an hour. (2000: http://www.science-spirit.org).

[13] I have discussed this process in detail elsewhere. Please refer to Forster 2005:29-44).

[14] Fr Bede was greatly influenced by Sri Aurobindo. Sri Aurobindo was a political activist and spiritual master who first came to prominence in India during India's struggle for independence from the British. Sri Aurobindo balanced social action and mystical contemplation in his spirituality. The following quote of Sri Aurobindo illustrates aptly his views on the evolution of consciousness.

There is an evolution of the consciousness behind the evolution of the species and this spiritual evolution must end in a realization, individual and collective, on the earth (in Judith, A 1996. "Sri Aurobindo" http://www.gaiamind.org).

[15] Wilber explains his theory of pluridimensional consciousness using a spectrum of consciousness. The spectrum of consciousness is a

... pluridimensional approach to man's identity; that is to say, each level of the Spectrum is marked by a different and easily recognized sense of individual identity, which ranges from Supreme identity of cosmic consciousness through several gradations or bands to the drastically narrowed sense of identity associated with egoic consciousness (Wilber 1975:106).

Adapted from Wilber 1975.

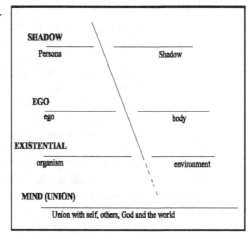

SHADOW

Persona   Shadow

EGO

ego   body

EXISTENTIAL

organism   environment

MIND (UNION)

Union with self, others, God and the world

[16] For a detailed discussion of perennial philosophy please see Forster
2006:172-174. Here is a basic definition of this philosophy:

> Perennial Philosophy is a term that is often used as a
> synonym for Santana Dharma (Sanskrit for "Eternal or
> Perennial Truth"). It was used by Leibniz to designate the
> common, eternal philosophy that underlies all religious
> movements, in particular the mystical streams within
> religions. The term was popularized by Aldous Huxley in his
> 1945 book The Perennial Philosophy in his description of
> Vedanta.
> (http://en.wikipedia.org/wiki/The_Perennial_Philosophy,
> accessed 4 July 2005, 12h41).

[17] Matthew Fox gives a detailed discussion of the biblical roots of the
doctrine of the cosmic Christ, both in the New and Old Testaments,
showing how it developed from the Old Testament understanding of
the relationship between creation and Creator, to the more technical
understanding of creation in, through, and for Christ, as found in the
Epistles. See Fox, M 1998 *The coming of the cosmic Christ : The
healing of Mother Earth and the birth of a global renaissance*. San
Francisco: Harper Collins. (pp..83-107).

[18] For a good synopsis on the stance of the Second Vatican Council in
relation to religious pluralism see Gaybba 1981:77-104.

[19] Sri Aurobindo also had a view of consciousness as evolutionary (also
see footnote 13 above). Judith comments on Sri Aurobindo's view in
the following manner:

> To him, the underlying thrust of the entire phenomenal
> world is a spiritual evolution in consciousness toward a
> situation in which all material forms will reveal the
> indwelling spirit. He postulated several states of
> consciousness, such as the Overmind, Intuitive mind, Higher
> mind, and Illumined mind. These states he saw as
> interconnected and revealing different levels of reality and
> unity. Normal waking consciousness is steeped in
> individualism, while the higher states reveal an ultimate
> unity. Psyche or soul was the manifestation of the divine as
> it occurs within individuals, for the purpose of reuniting
> with the universal (Judith, A 1996. "Sri Aurobindo"
> http://www.gaiamind.org).

[20] See also *The space in the heart of the lotus: Bede Griffiths a
Benedictine in India*. 1993. MTI Films, where Fr Bede uses this
illustration.

[21] This book has pointed out only those aspects of Christian theology that have directly informed Fr Bede's cosmic Christology. For a far more detailed and broader discussion on cosmic Christology and its significance for Christian theology see Lyons, JA 1982 *The cosmic Christ in Origen and Teilhard de Chardin*. Oxford: Oxford University Press.

[22] It needs to be mentioned, in order that the reader is not misled, that Fr Bede was well aware that the Hindu concept of *lila* had a greater meaning and significance than 'fun and games'. He writes:

> ...all activity is a lila, a play of God. This is the view of Ramakrishna. The great mother is playing, and all that goes on in this world is her play. By itself that is hardly satisfactory for it means that all the suffering of the world is ultimately meaningless. The concept of lila, however, can also be interpreted in the way towards which the Gita is working and which the modern Hindu certainly supports, namely that this lila of God has a meaning and purpose. In this view God is not merely at play but is purposefully active in the world.... This is consistent with the Christian understanding of the activity of God. The Crucifixion reveals that suffering is redemptive (1987:87).

[23] Sandra Schneiders, in her article *Spirituality in the academy*. (1990) names a number of theologians who are convinced that only theologies that are "rooted in the spiritual commitment of the theologian and oriented towards praxis will be meaningful in the Church of the future" (1990:17). These include theologians such as, Karl Rahner, Mary Collins, Charles Curran, Margaret Farley, Gustavo Guitierrez, Monika Hellwig, Hans Kung, Bernard Longeran, Rosemary Radford Reuther, Edward Schillebeeckx and Dorothee Soelle. The names of Raimundo Panikkar and Ewert Cousins, although not mentioned by Schneiders, can also be added to this list. In keeping with this line of argument one can cite Gustavo Gutierrez, the liberation theologian, who writes that it is from spirituality "that liberation theology emerges... [spirituality] represents... a deeper penetration of the very wellspring from which this kind of theological thinking flows" (Gutierrez 1988:xxxii).

[24] A popular scientific example of this effect can be found in the theories of the quantum physicist Schrödinger, and the analogy of 'Schrödinger's cat" (please see http://en.wikipedia.org/wiki/Schr%C3%B6dinger's_cat accessed 10.48, 16 October 2007).

Made in the USA
Middletown, DE
16 December 2023

45847333R00074